Pause. Reflect. Lead.

AF646871

Shyam Malhotra

ZORBA BOOKS

ZORBA BOOKS

Published by Zorba Books, December 2025
Website: www.zorbabooks.com
Email: info@zorbabooks.com
Author Name: Shyam Malhotra
Copyright ©: Shyam Malhotra

Title: Pause. Reflect. Lead.

Printbook ISBN: 978-93-5896-361-8
Ebook ISBN: 978-93-5896-746-3

All rights reserved. No part of this book may be reproduced or transmitted in any form or by any means, electronic or mechanical, except by a reviewer. The reviewer may quote brief passages, with attribution, in a review to be printed in a magazine, newspaper, or on the Web—without permission in writing from the copyright owner.

The publisher under the guidance and direction of the author has published the contents in this book, and the publisher takes no responsibility for the contents, its accuracy, completeness, any inconsistencies, or the statements made. The contents of the book do not reflect the opinion of the publisher or the editor. The publisher and editor shall not be liable for any errors, omissions, or the reliability of the contents of the book.

Any perceived slight against any person/s, place or organization is purely unintentional.

Zorba Books Pvt. Ltd. (opc)
Sushant Arcade,
Next to Courtyard Marriot,
Sushant Lok 1, Gurgaon – 122009, India

Printed in India

Contents

Acknowledgement .... *v*
Preface........ *vii*
About Shyam Malhotra........ *ix*

1. Belief and Reality........ 1
2. Mind Your Mindset........ 3
3. Being Judgemental 12
4. 40 to 50: Avoid the Trim List 15
5. 40 to 50: Caught in the Trim List?........ 19
6. To Err is Human 24
7. The Attached Observer........ 28
8. Curious and Concerned 31
9. Intuition Harnessing........ 34
10. Your Avatars and You........ 37
11. The Cheetah and the Chameleon........ 44
12. Talk the Walk 47
13. River, Dam and Leadership........ 51
14. Building Presence: Mindspace or Timespace?........ 53
15. Tyranny of Tools........ 56
16. Drowning in Self- Expectations?........ 59
17. Master of Expectation Management........ 63
18. Mirror, Mirror, on the Wall........ 67
19. Let Go – But of What? 70
20. Resume Plus 74
21. Power of Acceptance........ 78
22. Grow the Box 82
23. Confidence Plus........ 86
24. The Power of the Pause........ 94
25. Lessons From Rawat Ji........ 98
26. Twists, Turns and Success........ 102

27. The Myth of the Right Decision 107
28. Making the Decision Right 112
29. The Hard Part of Soft Skills 115
30. Being Firm and Gentle 120
31. Blues at Fifty 124
32. tsunAmI 130
33. The Stress Virus 137
34. Managing Your Ego Diet 143
35. Difficult Conversations Made Easy 146
36. The Clone 151
37. Resolutions! 155
38. The Art of Peer Management 159
39. Top Ten Self-Saboteurs 165
40. The Stool of Upsets 169
41. Tanya's Challenge: Building Senior Presence 176
42. PVR and the Drama Triangle 181
43. The Big Bad Boss 185
44. Feelings and Emoticons 189
45. The Impact of the Virus 192
46. The Rusted Blades 196
47. Success, Fulfilment, and AI 200
48. A Conversation with Claude.AI 203
49. Communicating for Impact 208
50. The Manager's Toolbox 212
51. Managing the Small, Sticky Stuff 217
52. The First Listener 223
53. Post-Reaction Recovery 228
54. Tanya's Legacy 234

Index of Thematic Ideas 239

Acknowledgement

This collection of selected articles is owed to all those who have taught me. And that is a lot of people. Because every interaction leaves a mark. Some of these marks you are conscious of. Others become sub conscious. But the etchings remain for all of them. My family, my friends, my acquaintances, my colleagues, my clients and my co-travellers. I owe you all. More than you know.

Through these essays I hope that I can share with others a small part of what I learnt from you.

Thank you.

Preface

This collection is for the managers and leaders caught in the busyness of output and outcomes. Through brief thoughtful essays it invites you to reflect on your patterns, recalibrate your responses and live and lead from a place of clarity and choice. These 53 pieces are a deck of thoughts for you. Pick and choose the hand you want to play.

Over fifty years of work - and seventy years of life - there are many learnings which have come my way. First as an executive, then as an entrepreneur and finally as an executive coach to senior leaders in global organisations. Some of these are captured in this collection. In each column there is an element of real-life situations. I have tried to capture the essence of over 5000 hours of coaching conversations and 30 years of work.

Each piece may seem unconnected but each is an observation of leadership skills and mindsets. Each fits into the gamut of infinite leadership situations. Situations which are frustrating and exhilarating at the same time. Situations which taught me as they taught others. Situations which need the stability of an elephant and the agility of a cat. Situations which are never linear. Situations which never have one correct decision. Situations which demand complete involvement from a place of detachment.

Take your time. Read a piece or two. Pause. Reflect. Chew on the learnings. Practice them. Adapt them. There is no specific order. There is no one right learning.

Mind Drops. Pebbles on the seashore. Stray Birds. Straws in the wind. Call them what you will. Make them into what you want. To the curious and reflective there is a lot to discover and link to your own experiences and journey.

Leaders and managers navigating change, team issues, personal inflection points in their careers – or life - will find the collection most useful. It will also be useful for executive coaches, HR professionals. And everybody else who lives on the intersection of work and life.

In a time deprived world brevity is a great virtue. But it cannot be at a cost of nuance and depth. Hence each piece seeks to be concise but layered - encouraging rereading and introspection. You will often be called to self-inquiry, nudging you to apply insights personally or professionally.

Because the real value is not in knowing more but in applying what you know.

On these pages you will find a rich tapestry of essays written in a style which is conversational and reflective, inviting the reader into a dialogue rather than delivering instruction. You will find the content rooted in real-world scenarios, coaching conversations, and everyday observations. Rich with metaphors and analogies the themes covered include leadership and management, mindset and self-awareness, coaching principles, workplace change and adaptability, career transitions, executive presence and impactful communication, navigating uncertainty and ambiguity, the art of influencing, managing self & stakeholders. And more.

About Shyam Malhotra

Shyam Malhotra is an executive coach, mentor, and leadership advisor who has spent over three decades helping individuals and organizations grow with clarity, calm, and authenticity. His journey bridges the worlds of corporate leadership and human development — a journey that began in boardrooms and now continues in reflective coaching conversations with senior leaders across sectors.

A former business leader with Siemens, Tata Exports, Cyber Media India Ltd., and Eicher Tractors, Shyam understands the complex realities of running large organizations, meeting targets, and leading teams through uncertainty. Yet, through years of observation and experience, he discovered a deeper truth — that leadership impact depends less on what we *know*, and more on how we *show up*.

Today, Shyam partners with senior executives, founders, and leadership teams to help them navigate complexity with composure. His approach blends structure and spontaneity — rigorous thinking with human warmth — creating space for insight, renewal, and authentic action.

Shyam believes that leadership begins with self-awareness. His coaching rests on a simple yet profound idea: that **our inner world shapes the outer results we create.**

He often describes emotions as *"uninvited guests"* — signals that knock on our door during stressful moments. Rather than resisting them, Shyam invites leaders to acknowledge these guests, understand what they bring, and learn to respond with choice instead of reaction.

His conversations are gentle yet searching, focused on bringing clarity where there is noise, and presence where there is pressure. Whether it is a CEO dealing with a demanding board, or a manager struggling with self-doubt, Shyam helps them reconnect with their sense of calm, purpose, and agency.

At the heart of his work lies a belief that **great leadership is not about control, but about coherence** — when thought, word, and action align, people begin to trust, follow, and grow.

His major work is in the areas of executive presence and impact, managing emotional triggers, transitioning to senior leadership roles, enhanced influence, impact communication & purposeful fulfilling leadership.

Shyam is an alumnus of **IIT Delhi** and **IIM Calcutta**. He is also a **Master Certified Coach (MCC)** – International Coaching Federation (ICF), a Marshall Goldsmith Stakeholder-Centred Coach and a Coach for Life (USA) graduate.

He can be reached at shyam@pobox.com or at +91 9811010093.

Belief and Reality

Strong belief systems fuel passion, purpose, and possibility, yet they're often dismissed as unrealistic or naive. This piece explores how belief—when guided by awareness—can be a powerful force for performance, even when others urge you to 'get real'.

I Think I Can, But…

As an executive coach, I often come across clients with strong beliefs. These beliefs encompass their aspirations, approaches to tasks, and perceptions of how the organisation should function, among other things. When they share their beliefs, their body language shifts — they sit up straight, their voices are filled with passion, and their tone generates energy.

However, many of these clients also express frustrations. Their beliefs are perceived as 'not real' by their managers and colleagues. Their expectations are dismissed as 'far-fetched', and their analyses of organisational situations are labelled as 'fuzzy'. They are often urged to 'get real' and to factor in 'reality' to establish achievable goals, to exceed targets, optimise resources, increase productivity, and boost stock prices.

Belief is a far greater enabler than it is often given credit for. Clients with strong beliefs tend to deliver more value—for themselves and for their organisations. Their 'far-fetched expectations' reflect their above- average ambitions while their perceived 'fuzziness' allows them to envision a broader range of possibilities.

Belief brings commitment, passion, energy, excitement, and possibilities. Reality, on the other hand, introduces doubts, precautions, safety nets, comfort zones, and constraints. The challenge for managers is to align these two aspects and ensure that acknowledging reality does not lead to a suspension of belief.

Mind Your Mindset

Our mindsets shape how we see ourselves and the world around us. Some mindsets empower us, while others limit us. This piece explores how to identify and question unhelpful mental patterns, enabling a shift toward liberating, growth-oriented perspectives that support change.

Mindsets can behave like bullies—they persistently bother you until confronted, at which point they tend to fade away. As human beings, we cannot operate without mindsets—claiming to have an 'open mind' is itself a mindset. Thus, the objective is to transition from negative, discouraging, and opposing mindsets to positive, encouraging, and supportive ones.

Like talents and abilities, mindsets can be acquired, altered, and transitioned. One effective method to achieve this is by relentlessly questioning these mindsets. Many negative mindsets are formed based on experiences and inputs accumulated over many years. Not all those learnings were correct or relevant, yet they remain, much like loyal but unhelpful friends. Asking oneself penetrating, thoughtful questions is a powerful tool to address these mental fault lines.

Questions can help identify mindsets that require transition, as well as facilitate it. Most of these questions are directed inward, although friends and family can serve as sounding boards—provided they are genuine sounding boards and not echo chambers that simply validate one's beliefs because it is comfortable to do so.

Some discomfort is natural in the process of converting limiting thoughts into liberating ones.

Here are some generic questions to consider:

1. Am I willing to endure that period?
2. What is this mindset about? How can it be described? Can I summarise it in a few words? For example, 'In my mind, making a big career transition is not for me.'
3. Is this mindset supported by real data, facts, or examples?
4. When did I last make a change? What challenges did I face? How do people like me successfully make such transitions, and do they succeed?

5. Is there an alternative interpretation for these facts? Could it be that the difficulties I faced in the past are no longer applicable? Am I stronger and more equipped now?
6. What is the mindset doing for me? What am I gaining from it? What could I be losing? If I don't make the transition, will I risk stagnation or even termination? Am I gaining short- term comfort, and is it realistic to think that this will continue?
7. What would I lose if this mindset disappeared? What could I gain? If I begin believing that I am as capable as anyone else of making a transition, how would my situation change? What would I gain or lose?

There are many more questions to ponder, but these should be sufficient to get the mind working.

Broadly speaking, mindsets can be categorised into limiting ones and liberating ones.

Examples of limiting mindsets include statements such as:

- I have tried everything.
- I know this will not happen.
- Tell me what is the use of changing things?
- I do not think I can change now.
- This old way is the best way forward.
- Experience is a valuable quality that I must always respect.
- People do not understand how this really works.
- The quality of inputs is low these days.
- My team is not good enough; I really need to get new people in.
- Under the given conditions, I am doing the best I can.

Examples of liberating mindsets include statements such as:

- What have I not yet tried yet?
- There is more to be tried.
- I cannot decide if it will happen or not until I have tried it.
- Change is good for the human body, mind, and spirit.
- Experience must be honoured, not worshipped.
- I may not change, but trying is a must.
- Most people are helpful and understanding.
- I cannot control what comes to me – I can impact what goes from me.
- I am doing my best. Now how can I improve?

Identifying which of these statements you associate with and use frequently can provide insight into your typical mindsets. It also empowers you to confront or modify them.

As an executive coach, I frequently observe typical mindsets that people operate with. *Understanding and shifting these internal orientations can profoundly influence your leadership, collaboration, and personal growth.*

Here are some specific limiting and liberating mindsets that frequently occur in the workplace. I have encountered these frequently in my fifteen plus years of coaching senior executives in multiple organisations.

Abundance Mindset vs. Scarcity Mindset

An abundance mindset manifests as 'I have enough'. Ideas, resources, time, people, knowledge, and skills are all viewed as plentiful, leading to a sense of comfort, security, and a willingness to embrace change. It encourages generosity and sharing, fostering a sense of fulfilment.

In contrast, a scarcity mindset manifests as 'There is not enough'. Time feels limited and competition fierce, leading to the need for self-protection and a reluctance to share. This mindset often results in perpetual dissatisfaction.

Solution Mindset vs. Problem Mindset

A solution-oriented mindset manifests as 'There has to be a better way to do this – and I can find it'. This mindset focuses on solutions, seeks common ground for collaboration, and possesses high self-belief. It does not define and then redefine the problem. It is willing to implement solutions swiftly and views every small contribution as progress.

Conversely, a problem-focused mindset comes from a very analytical mind and tends to dissect and redefine the complexity of issues in detail, often losing sight of potential solutions. It may typically manifest in statements like 'The problem is that....', 'We need to be careful ...', 'Let us look at what all can go wrong ....', 'Is this worth the risk', 'Let us first do the present job well', or 'What can I do alone?'

Climb Mindset vs. Cruise Mindset

When individuals adopt a climb mindset, they actively seek growth – material, emotional, or physical. Individuals with this mindset strive to make each day better than the last, set targets, upgrade their skills, and embrace challenges. They feel compelled to push harder when faced with setbacks, keeping their focus on forward and upward movement.

On the other hand, a cruise mindset reflects a maintenance mode. While individuals with this mindset may not wish to lose progress, they are content with a lack of growth. This mindset often values fulfilment over success and may prioritise spirituality over material gain. Many may consider this a liberating mindset.

However, another form of the cruise mindset can involve a passive approach to growth. Individuals with this mindset like to leave it to someone else to make growth happen and blame external circumstances for their stagnation. They may display behaviours associated with cruise but have the wish list of a climber. This mindset can lead to frustration.

Owner Mindset vs. Worker Mindset

An owner mindset is grounded in accountability. Individuals with this mindset take full responsibility for their job. They do not wait to be told what to do; they actively seek out answers and are willing to go the extra mile, finding satisfaction in their work ethic and achievements, without worrying about the short- term rewards.

In contrast, a worker mindset often requires clear instructions and guidance from a supervisor. Individuals with this mindset prefer their roles and responsibilities, as well as working hours, holidays, and incentives to be defined. Having supervision and clear instructions on what to do and when to do it makes them feel secure and comfortable. Their satisfaction is derived from external validation and monetary rewards. They thrive only within clear boundaries, as they believe this is the correct approach.

Victim Mindset vs. Creator Mindset

Individuals with a victim mindset feel discriminated against. They view the system as unfair to them and often think they receive the toughest assignments with minimal support. They are of the view that their superior appears to listen to others but ignores their concerns. External circumstances also seem to conspire against them. They feel they give their best effort but receive the worst outcomes in return. While the qualifications of others are valued, their experience is overlooked. They are of the view that they work in very difficult conditions and feel misunderstood. They feel they often carry the burden for others who do not contribute equally. These thoughts are typical of a victim mindset.

Conversely, individuals with a creator mindset realise that the environment is the same for everyone. They believe it is up to them to harness it. They strive to communicate better if others do not understand them. Sometimes they have good breaks and sometimes bad ones. They are of the view that everyone is like them – they do their best, and sometimes it does not work out. They believe that people, in general, are fair and appreciate good work, even if it is not explicitly acknowledged. The system applies to everyone–some learn to navigate it, while others do not. Over time, the effort- reward ratio tends to even out. These thoughts are indicative of a creator mindset.

Big Picture Mindset vs. Small Picture Mindset

Individuals with a big picture mindset ask themselves the following questions:

- What perspective am I adopting in my mind?
- Does it provide a wide- angle, inclusive view of the current challenge?
- Do I view challenges with a broader visionary approach?
- Am I knowledgeable about all aspects of the project?
- Am I more focused on the result or on the minor details?
- Do I pursue big goals, trusting that the details will take care of themselves?

On the other hand, individuals with a small picture mindset ask themselves the following questions:

- Is my perspective too narrow, emphasising details at the expense of the bigger picture?
- Am I so blinded by the current concerns and so detailed- oriented that I end up being a micro manager?
- Do I need reports on everything from everyone?
- Do I believe that the "devil is in the details"?
- Do I feel the need to verify every aspect personally?

Team Mindset vs. Individual Mindset

Individuals with a team mindset strongly believe that their success is tied to that of the team. They value sharing credit with others and adhere to the principle that "a chain is only as strong as its weakest link". They enjoy helping those who approach them for problem- solving.

Conversely, individuals with an individual mindset do not interfere in others' areas. They feel they would be exploited if they help too much. While teams are necessary, individuals matter most. They believe that their job is to do their best; others need to handle their own responsibilities. They are of the view that in general, people cannot be trusted; they only trust those whom they have known for years. They believe they must look out for themselves.

Security Mindset vs. Risk Mindset

A security-oriented mindset emphasises caution and careful planning. They believe it is important to consider what can go wrong before deciding. They believe there is limited need to change, and tried and trusted methods work best. Experience teaches what is right and wrong; the known devil is better than the unknown one are their strong beliefs.

In contrast, those with a risk-oriented mindset believe that the biggest risk is not taking risks at all. Dynamic business conditions require constant change. They enjoy the challenge of trying new things and learn from experience. They believe that if no one took risks, there would be stagnation.

You may want to now decide which mindsets you want to work on and transition to the liberating ones.

Being Judgemental

Judging others often masquerades as helpful feedback, but it rarely helps. This piece explores the difference between being judgemental and exercising discernment, and why self-awareness, empathy, and timing are crucial. It aims to identify common traps and provide ways to reframe your responses to build better relationships.

Stop Being Judgemental!

We frequently hear the phrase "Don't be judgemental". But what does it really mean? Is it the same as never making a judgement? Clearly not.

Making a judgement stems from a neutral, balanced outlook. It involves a holistic view and considers the principle of materiality. Often, a judgement is made with a soft and supportive approach, coming from a place of genuine concern.

In contrast, being judgemental comes from an opinionated mindset. It lacks a holistic understanding and overlooks the complete context surrounding the person being judged. It often manifests as nitpicking and can include an undertone of "I told you so". Self-righteousness is a defining characteristic of a judgemental person. While there may be concern for the other person, it usually does not come across that way.

Being judgemental can damage relationships and have far-reaching negative effects in various aspects of work and life. It risks missing out on valuable inputs and enriching conversations. For some, such encounters can leave a lingering bad taste long after the moment has passed.

So, why do all of us become judgemental, at least occasionally?

Here are some reasons to consider. How many do you recognise in yourself?

1. A strong sense of right and wrong, leaving no middle ground for complex situations
2. Viewing situations in black and white, expecting constant consistency from others
3. Feeling the need to appear knowledgeable and offer input—broadly termed as ego

4. An inability to admit that one may be wrong
5. An overdeveloped sense of responsibility, believing, "If I do not point this out, who will?"
6. A belief that one knows more (or is supposed to know more) and therefore must correct others
7. A sense of disbelief that others cannot understand something one finds simple
8. A desire to win arguments at all costs
9. A need to protect oneself from being hurt
10. Insecurity or feelings of inferiority, leading to attempts to boost one's self- worth
11. A victim mentality, perceiving others as threats that need to be addressed pre-emptively
12. Difficulty in recognising the positive traits in people. Try making a list of positive attributes for a couple of individuals. How easy or difficult was that?
13. Catching oneself thinking, "How can anyone be like that?"
14. A low sense of self-worth, sometimes disguised as being overly busy with tasks
15. Saying the right thing in the wrong way

As the saying goes, "Do not judge a book by its cover." At the very least, browse through the contents page! If you can do this for a book, why not extend the same effort for a human being?

40 to 50: Avoid the Trim List

Are you in your 40s or 50s and working in a corporate role? This is your call to action. Learn how to future-proof your career, demonstrate value beyond your experience, and avoid becoming invisible. This is essential reading for those wanting to stay off the dreaded "trim list".

If you are in this age group and working in a large corporation, you are likely to have heard about layoffs. Organisations – especially MNCs – implement layoffs regularly. While your organisation may not have downsized yet or you may not be on the trim list, it's wise to remain vigilant for potential warning signs. One thing is certain: if you are in this age group and get laid off, it will be challenging to find new options unless you are prepared. As a career transition coach, I have worked with numerous individuals who unfortunately found themselves on the trim list.

I can say with certainty that they were not actively trying to avoid this outcome. If they had been, they may not have needed my assistance.

Here are some warning signs to look out for:

1. Lack of Key Attributes: Wittingly or unwittingly, you may not have demonstrated the essential skills needed for higher or lateral options in your organisation. These skills include strategic thinking, leadership presence, collaboration based on relationships, external presence and networking, influencing skills, managing peer groups, excellent communication skills, motivational leadership, quick learning, agility, and adaptability. Note that these are not knowledge or experience- dependent attributes; they are skills or competencies. The key word here is "demonstrate". You may believe that you possess these skills, but have you actively showcased them? Have you used them for organisational advantage? Have you been acknowledged for them? If not, now is the time to start focusing on them.
2. Growth Mindset: You may not have exhibited a growth mindset or ambition to move beyond your current role.

Remember, excelling at your job is not the same as showing a desire to grow beyond it. Have you invested in your development? Do you seek to learn new things? Are you interested in other departments within your organisation? Do you ask questions, show interest, or offer suggestions beyond your immediate duties? Do you actively seek challenging assignments? Have you inquired about what is needed for your growth? Your development is your responsibility, not that of HR, your manager, or anyone else.

3. Value Addition: If your compensation has increased in recent years while your contribution to the organisation has remained relatively unchanged, you may be at risk of being on the trim list. Others doing similar work for significantly less pay is also a red flag.
4. Organisational Changes: If your organisation is undergoing a strategic shift—such as new product lines, a new management team, or changes in geographic focus—you may find yourself outside of your area of expertise. It's vital to stay informed about these changes and articulate your willingness to learn and adapt, or you risk being added to the trim list.
5. Stalled Career Progression: In the last few years, if your peers have advanced while you have remained in the same position, it's worth asking yourself why this has happened. What did they do that you did not? What opportunities did they seize that you missed? More importantly, what actions can you take now to facilitate your own career advancement?
6. Overvaluing Experience: While experience and loyalty are certainly valuable, they become less significant in periods of rapid change. Industries like IT, communications, and banking have historically seen

this, and new sectors such as automotive, energy, and e-commerce are now experiencing similar shifts. Avoid overvaluing your experience and underestimating the importance of your strengths, current skills, and the need for continual evolution. Try talking for a few minutes about your strengths, skills, and contributions to the organisation without mentioning your experience. How easy is that for you?

7. Comfort in Established Roles: If you are most comfortable in large organisations where roles are predefined and assigned, you may be limiting your growth potential. Yes, many large companies function this way, and it can work well in stable economic conditions. However, to thrive in a dynamic environment, consider becoming a role maker rather than a role taker. Identify where you can add value, potentially even in entirely different functions. Have you recognised these opportunities? Have you pursued them? This approach can often help you avoid the trim list.

I am sure there are other strategies as well. But are you actively seeking them out?

It is always better to be safe than sorry!

40 to 50: Caught in the Trim List?

Have you got caught in the Trim List? Being on the trim list can feel like a shock—especially after years of loyal contribution. Here's a practical, clear-eyed guide to help you regroup, reframe, and reorient your career with purpose and agility.

So you got caught on the trim list. And have been given some time to find yourself a new career opportunity. You have been with the organisation for some time, doing reasonably well so this is a surprise. You did not think that this would happen to you. You are somewhat angry – certainly disappointed. Thanks to a generous package you have some time available but would like to get going as soon as possible. You have a work experience of 25 odd years and this period you have grown well. You are proud of your achievements. But now feeling whether all that loyalty was worthwhile.

What next? Here are a few thoughts which emerge from the Career Transition Coaching that I offer to people.

1. To start with try not to blame yourself. Organisations 'right size' for many reasons. Your performance is not always the reason for being asked to move on. Rarely it is an individual based decision. It has more to do with strategic changes, overall company performance, new organisational structure, new manager etc. Yes – you could have done some things differently to cut down this probability. But now is not a good time for that contemplation.
2. Have a close look at your resume. A good resume should reflect what you are good at, how did you use those skills and what was the impact on the organisation. It does not have to be a chronological listing of your experience. Experience is just a surrogate measure. Two people with the same experience can have completely different skill sets. You get hired for what you can do for the new organisation using these skill sets – not for your past experience. Try to highlight that. And – keep it short. Two pages at the maximum – of a clean readable format. You will be surprised by the number of resumes

that I have seen which do not fit these conditions. Type in 'how to write a good resume' on Google and you will get many more ideas.

3. Research the job that you are applying for. Find out what the job needs. And try to see how you can value add to it. You may have to craft your message individually for each job. One resume does not fit all. You can change the resume or add a specific covering note for each opening that you are applying for. At senior levels the profile is often sent after initial discussions take place on phone or in person. That gives a chance to find out more and customise the resume.
4. At senior levels openings get filled through networks. So you have to activate / reactivate your network. Reach out to as many people as you can. Make sure that your profile has reached placement agencies. Make a list of organisations who could use your services – competitors, dealers, suppliers, customers – and see how you can reach out to them. There is no right number – so the more you activate the network the higher the probability of success. This can feel odd at times. How do I ask people that I need a job? But please do remember that most people want to help. If someone approached you would you be helping or laughing? Well – good news is that most people are like you.
5. Use contemporary words / terms in your profile. Similar job profiles are described differently. Your profile should use present day descriptions.
6. Get active on linked in. More and more jobs are being sourced through linked in. If you are not active this is a good time to start. There are enough articles / videos available on how to use linked in better. Invest some time there. It will be useful.

7. For each discussion / contact you must ask the question – how can I value add to this job? And you must find every possible opportunity to state that. The first question – 'tell us about yourself' does not need your life history. Just a bit of that – and then 'I think I can do …. for this job'
8. If you are at senior levels compensation in the new job could be an issue. You may be overpriced for the market. Break up your compensation into fixed and variable and start with the fixed and negotiate up. Starting with the total high figure scares some organisations.
9. Large organisations of the type that you have been working in are not the universe of options. Medium or small organisations may have greater need for your expertise. However, they would not be able to pay as much. So you may need to be flexible for other options like ESOPs, profit linked compensation etc. They would also, in most cases, want you to contribute in a significant way to the build the business. You would have to demonstrate interest in and have ability to go beyond a functional area. And of course their culture and operating style is different. Remain flexible. Build agility. This is most often a mindset issue.
10. A job may not be the only career available for you. The closer you are to fifty the hiring process becomes more difficult to surmount. So what is your Plan B? Advisor, consultant, entrepreneur, early retirement? There could be many options to consider. Simply because you have not thought of these earlier does not make them bad options. In considering such options is making a re- assessment of the financial needs. What is the corpus you need? And how close are you to it?

> Have worked with many people and greater than 70 percent have not done this assessment at all or done it incorrectly. People have assets which they have built up for tough times. But during tough times they would like to hang to them – for tougher times!

For many people that I have worked with the layoff has been a blessing in disguise. Without realising they were caught in the humdrum of corporate life. The invisible golden handcuffs were doing their role to perfection. The jolt gave them a chance to things that they really wanted to do. Examples – one has to gone abroad to complete a doctorate, another one has started a hiking tours company, one has gone off into the food business and a couple have decided to become coaches!

As poet Iqbal says 'Sitaron Ke Aage Jahan Aur Bhi Hain'.

There are worlds beyond the stars.

To Err is Human

Envy, revenge, and regret—three emotions people are reluctant to admit to. Yet, these emotions silently shape our behaviour, drain our energy, and undermine our leadership. This article explores how to recognise these 'hidden drivers' within us or others and why identifying them is key to moving past them.

We all know that underlying feelings and emotions drive observable behaviour. As a coach, it is important to help individuals identify these emotions.

Among the most challenging emotions to recognise in ourselves are envy, revenge, and regret, which we often deny because of their negative nature. As a result, behaviours stemming from these emotions can be difficult to address.

This energy-draining behaviour can lead the person exhibiting it to become obsessed and unable to concentrate on constructive work. For those on the receiving end, it can cause feelings of anger, resentment, or confusion. Recognising these emotions—especially within ourselves—is critical.

Here are a few ways these emotions may manifest:

Envy

Envy often appears in the form of:

- Disparaging comments about someone in meetings
- Ignoring well-meaning inputs from others
- Failing to acknowledge someone's achievements, or doing so only as a formality
- Displaying curt or rude behaviour
- Giving backhanded compliments
- Avoiding a person altogether

Interestingly, envy can also drive individuals to strive to be like the person they envy, all the while pretending to be someone entirely different. The first place to look for envy is among peers, managers, friends, and sometimes even juniors in the workplace.

Are you envious of certain people? It would be surprising if you weren't at some point. Take a moment to reflect on how that feeling affects you. Remember, being envious is different from being competitive.

Revenge

Behaviours motivated by revenge tend to be more intense. They can involve brooding, planning, or conspiring to discredit or sabotage others. Those who exhibit such behaviour feel wronged and may frequently discuss the injustices they perceive. Revenge-driven behaviour often targets managers or senior staff and may manifest as:

- Passive aggression
- Ignoring instructions
- Gloating over others' misfortunes
- Making "I told you so" remarks
- Complaining about a person to others or higher authorities
- Creating obstacles for another person's work
- Bad- mouthing an individual
- Making fun of a person

In rare cases, this behaviour can become vicious, sometimes extending to entire departments or organisations.

If you catch yourself engaging in any of these behaviours, it may indicate feelings of revenge, something that many people struggle to accept. Is this occurring in your life? What emotions does this elicit for you?

Regret

Regret often follows envious or vengeful behaviours. It might surface immediately after the act or after a period of time, sometimes buried deep but festering beneath the surface.

Individuals experiencing regret may feel bad about themselves, their self-esteem can plummet, and they might become overly nice as compensation. Conversely, they may try to avoid the person associated with their feelings of regret. Living with regret can drain a person's energy and lead to serious consequences over time.

Living with envy, revenge, or regret is not healthy. Unfortunately, much like depression, these emotions often go unrecognised and are frequently denied. Coaches are often called upon to help clients cope with the outcomes of this unholy trinity.

As always, it's vital for the coach to avoid passing judgment.

After all, to err is human.

The Attached Observer

Can you be deeply present with someone without getting entangled? This article introduces the concept of the 'Attached Observer'—a coach or anyone else who fully senses another person but responds with detachment and clarity. This meditative and nuanced take on coaching presence can help in leadership development.

The term "detached observer" typically refers to a state where one perceives themselves as an outsider, seeing and hearing from a distant observation point, without involvement.

But what if I could be an "attached observer", especially in my coaching practice? Fully involved, engaged, and present—yet still just an observer. I would feel what the client is experiencing, understand their thoughts, and comprehend what is not immediately obvious, all without judgements, biases, filters, or emotions.

Do I need to learn something new to achieve this, or do I need to let go of everything I know? Do I need to reach a state of having no ego, no experience, no beliefs, and no agenda? There would be no need to provide solutions or to prove anything to anyone, including myself.

The *Sadhana*

I am sure there are many practices to facilitate this state. Here are three that work for me. It is important to note that this is a constant *Sadhana*—a practice without an end.

1. Observe and Sense: Pay attention to every little word, nuance, twitch of the eyebrow, and expression. However, observation alone is not enough. It must be supported by a layer of sensing—the ability to understand the unsaid and what lies behind the spoken words.
2. Zoom In, Zoom Out: Like a walkabout lens on a camera, I need to practice the ability to zoom in closely to the conversation and then zoom out to gain clarity. This process should be repeated multiple times during a single conversation.

3. Water off my Back: Engage with the conversation without being swept away by it—like a duck that floats on water without getting wet. I need my own versions of this ability.

Is it truly possible to be an attached observer? What other practices could help achieve this state?

Curious and Concerned

"Be empathetic" is a phrase we often hear, but how can we achieve this? Empathy is not just a warm feeling; it's about behaviour. This article explores two simple yet powerful ways to demonstrate empathy in action: curiosity and concern. It provides practical guidance for anyone looking to build deeper connections at work or in life.

We have all heard that being empathetic is crucial for understanding people and creating great teams. But how can I actually display empathy? After all, empathy is fundamentally a feeling, and feelings need to be expressed for others to perceive them.

From my experience, two actions that effectively convey empathy are being curious and being concerned.

Be Curious: Ask questions about the person's background, thoughts, beliefs, plans, habits, knowledge, family, problems, and solutions—whatever is relevant to the conversation. There is no better way to understand where someone is coming from, and this does not require much time or effort. Four or five thoughtful questions often suffice, and most people respond with answers that take just a minute or two.

Be Concerned: The act of asking questions also demonstrates your concern and interest in the other person. Concern can also be shown through silence—just ensure that you are fully present. Remaining silent does not mean switching off. Simple phrases like "I understand" or "I get that", accompanied by a nod, can also express concern. Sharing a similar experience occasionally can help, as long as it's done in a way that doesn't overshadow their feelings. Offering help in a non-judgemental manner and sharing useful information are also effective ways to display concern.

It's important to be aware of non-verbal signals as well. Your eyes can convey concern, while unintentional signs can broadcast a lack of interest. Are your shoulders shrugging involuntarily, your eyes rolling, or your gaze directed towards your smartphone or into the distance? Yawning or checking your watch sends a clear "I don't care" message.

Finally, genuineness is crucial. You cannot fake curiosity and concern for long; people sense a lack of interest much quicker than they sense genuine empathy. It's simply part of being human.

Intuition Harnessing

In a data-driven world, intuition often takes a back seat. Yet, intuitive judgement, when trusted and cultivated, offers insights where facts fall short. This article explores practical ways to recognise, nurture, and act upon your intuitive voice—especially when navigating uncertainty, complexity, or high-stakes decisions.

In a world of information overload, intuition struggles to make its presence felt.

In a world of information overload, intuition struggles to make its presence felt. Albert Einstein said, "The only real valuable thing is intuition." This remains true today.

Decisions are typically driven by information—data, facts, numbers, and research are used for decision-making. However, there are situations where information is scarce, yet decisions still need to be made. This is where intuition comes into play. If managers can learn to trust it, intuition can be a powerful guide. Unlike processed information, intuition must be trusted, and that trust must be built.

Consider these scenarios:

1. A junior member of the team has been irresponsible, and the data supports this conclusion. However, how much 'irresponsibility' is enough reason for termination?
2. You are negotiating with a difficult client, and negotiations are on the verge of breaking down. There is no more data to rely upon, and you cannot read the client's mind.

So how can one develop intuition?

1. Patience: Intuitive answers often come in a flash, but the timing of this flash is unpredictable. Intuitive ideas come to you; you do not actively seek them out.
2. Clarity of distance: Move away from the decision. The perspective gained from a distance can often provide clarity. Ask yourself, if someone else were making this decision, what would they do?

3. Rumination: Wonder about the people, trends, and situations involved in the decision—without a specific agenda. General thinking can sometimes lead to specific insights.
4. Silent Stillness: Create a conducive environment for your intuition to thrive. Quieting the mind allows space for intuitive thoughts. Engage in activities that work for you—meditation, listening to music, walking, or playing.
5. Feel the Decision: Getting in touch with your feelings is essential. If something doesn't feel right, it probably isn't. Trust that instinct.
6. Express Yourself: Intuition is a feeling that needs to be articulated. Just as thoughts become paintings on canvas, express your feelings through writing, doodling, sketching, or speaking. Capturing intuitive thoughts through expression prevents them from fading away.
7. Dig into the Past: Revisiting similar experiences can trigger ideas relevant to your current decisions.
8. Recognise it: Intuition can manifest in various forms—a sudden thought, a feeling of discomfort in your stomach, or an excitement coursing through your body. All these sensations can be clues.
9. Trust yourself: Have confidence in your ability to manage the consequences of the decisions you make. Only then can you take tough decisions in uncertain conditions.

While you cannot blindly follow intuition, you also cannot ignore it. As Jiddu Krishnamurthy states, "Intuition is the whisper of the soul."

Your Avatars and You

Every leader presents multiple faces—avatars that emerge at different times. Some drive success, while others can quietly derail it. This engaging piece explores over twenty leadership archetypes, helping you reflect on your dominant modes and discover which personas to amplify and which ones to gently retire.

All leaders possess various avatars within them, manifesting in different ways, sometimes consciously and sometimes subconsciously.

As a leader, can you recognise your most visible avatars? These are the ones on display most frequently. Identifying them can reveal great enablers as well as potential derailers. Sometimes your avatars support one another; at other times, they may pull you in conflicting directions.

Would it not be beneficial to recognise your avatars and make them work together?

Here are a few leadership avatars - modelled after real people I have had the opportunity to coach. See which ones resonate with you and which you would like to develop or retire. Note that this list is illustrative; you can define your own avatars, as there are many variations, much like avatars of the gods.

1. The Leading Light: You are the hero of the narrative. You make things happen effortlessly, and you are popular, with many talents that allow you to solve problems easily. People aspire to be like you, and you dominate most scenarios. You struggle to accept roles in which you are not the hero.
2. The Puppeteer: You are the one who holds all the strings behind the scenes. Your dexterity allows you to weave great stories and control the narrative. However, your followers lack their own agency—without you, they are lifeless and uninspired.
3. The Eveready Energiser: You are the battery that lights up situations with your humour, wisdom, solutions, creativity, and more. You don't need anyone to switch you on; you are always ready to engage. You don't mind shining a light on situations, people, and problems,

but sometimes you forget that the battery needs to be charged, or it can run down irrevocably.

4. The Mover and Shaker: You are always on the go, and you must always have something to do, accomplish, solve, or create. You are a self-starter, going to bed with a dozen ideas swirling in your mind and waking up with even more. If you don't have something to keep you occupied, you can become impatient, angry, and frustrated—traits that others may find difficult to tolerate.
5. The Future Perfect: You want the future to be perfect. You meticulously plan for all contingencies and have a keen eye for detail. One backup is never enough for you. You see beyond the obvious in most situations. You like to review your plans multiple times to cover all angles, but this can lead to agonising over decisions indefinitely
6. The Trouble Shooter: You are focused and capable of solving most problems. Routine tasks are mundane for you, as you come alive during a crisis. Otherwise, you would rather be somewhere more engaging
7. The Ringmaster: You enjoy being in the limelight and being the centre of attention. You oversee everything happening around you, adapting to various roles—from taming tigers to playing the clown. You maintain control and ensure that everything runs smoothly, even if that means cracking the whip for effect.
8. The Trapeze Artist: Precision, smoothness, and a strong sense of balance are your special skills. You thrive at heights that might daunt others and can transition effortlessly from one task to another. Teamwork is a virtue you embrace; you prefer to come in, perform your act, take a bow, and return when needed.

9. The Perfectionist: You notice the slightest imperfections—a slightly tilted frame on the wall demands your attention. Disorder bothers you, and you believe that an ordered world is essential. While you may produce exceptional work, it can take you a long time to finish—long after the deadline has come and gone.
10. The Joker: For you, work is enjoyable, or you excel at making it look that way. You don't mind if people laugh with you or at you, as you distinguish between playing the fool and being a fool. You are a master of disguise, with your true self well concealed, preferring to nurse your wounds in solitude.
11. The Rebel: Being contrarian is your instinctive response. You enjoy questioning norms, pushing boundaries, and challenging the status quo. The old ways feel tiresome and useless to you, and you often feel compelled to shake things up, sometimes aggressively. Others may find you difficult to work with, but you are someone who gets things done.
12. The Navigator: You know the routes, have the maps, and are aware of shortcuts and obstacles along the way. You are alert and watchful, capable of sensing things on the road. While you can be patient and provide detailed yet precise directions, you prefer not to bear the responsibility of driving yourself.
13. The Buck Stopper: You embody responsibility; you welcome it eagerly, taking on tasks—sometimes even those not assigned to you. The buck stops with you. As the one who shoulders all duties, you will not rest until you fulfil every commitment. Headache pills often accompany you as your trusted companions.

14. Symphony Conductor: You are the person who brings everything together. You understand the nuances, set the tempo, and unify the team, controlling the pace of the performance. While you may not excel at playing any specific instrument, you possess the experience, mindfulness, and sensitivity to make all the instruments play harmoniously.
15. The Great Charmer: You easily build rapport with others, captivating them with your storytelling and ability to make them laugh. You remember names and faces, always knowing what to say at the right moment. You can initiate projects with enthusiasm and engage many people. However, you often struggle to bring these projects to completion as your attention shifts to new challenges.
16. The Preserver: You see little reason to change anything that isn't broken, and if something is broken, your first instinct is to fix it. You value preserving the old ways of working, ancient files, ideas that have stood the test of time, and the stories of the past. The past is your loyal friend, even if the world around you has moved on.
17. The Comfortable Collaborator: You are the quintessential team player—always ready to help and never afraid to ask for assistance. You freely share ideas and resources and are always there to support your colleagues. For you, the team is more important than the individual, and the only goals worth achieving are those of the team. Unfortunately for you, not all team members share the same mindset.
18. The Solution Provider: You have a strong inclination to offer solutions, whether they are practical or not. Helping others find answers is your motto, and you readily provide input. This approach works most of

the time—except when others simply want to talk and prefer to discover the answers on their own.

19. The Logic Lover: Data, numbers, proof, and facts are your lifeblood. You thrive on them and are ready to move mountains when a logical argument is presented. Conversely, you feel lost in the absence of concrete evidence and are uncomfortable with ambiguity. Shades of grey are not your strong suit.
20. Blender: You are the blender, skilfully mixing diverse elements into cohesive teams. You have a range of strengths and expect the same from others. You seamlessly blend into the team, prioritising group objectives over individual recognition. As a result, you may find that your contributions go unnoticed.
21. The Risk Calculator: You firmly believe in taking risks, but only when they are calculated. You meticulously evaluate all decision variables and potential outcomes, often focusing on the cost of failure rather than the profit of success. Uncertainty makes you uncomfortable, prompting you to take your time when making decisions. This caution can sometimes lead to missed opportunities. Your motto is "Better safe than sorry".
22. The Rock: You are a constant presence—grounded and unwavering. With a stoic demeanour, you remain unaffected by your surroundings. You dislike change and risks. You are always there for people when they need support.
23. The Banyan Tree: You envision yourself as the central trunk of a banyan tree, which spreads branches and spawns many roots. Each branch maintains its own identity while remaining connected to others, creating a big family. This model works well until a member seeks complete independence and transformation into a different type of tree.

If you recognise some of these traits in yourself, that's great! You can also look at the people around you and see their avatars. Understanding both your own traits and those of others can enhance your ability to manage interpersonal dynamics more effectively.

The Cheetah and the Chameleon

Agility and adaptability—represented by the cheetah's speed and the chameleon's sensitivity respectively—are no longer optional; they are essential for leadership in today's volatile, uncertain world. This article explores these twin traits and offers insights on how to cultivate them in your mindset, allowing you to move quickly and adapt smartly.

Both the cheetah and the chameleon exhibit qualities that are crucial in our VUCA (Volatility, Uncertainty, Complexity, and Ambiguity) world, which can often feel overwhelming. The cheetah can reach speeds of nearly 90 kilometres per hour in just 3-4 seconds. When it sprints, it is intensely focused on its prey, moving with powerful grace and perfect balance, courtesy of its heavy tail. It maintains high speeds—exceeding 100 kilometres per hour—even while executing sharp turns and can spot its prey from as far away as 5 kilometres.

In contrast, the chameleon has the remarkable ability to blend in and adapt as needed. It possesses eyes that can roll within their sockets, giving it nearly 360-degree vision, contributing to the belief that chameleons have eyes in the back of their heads. Additionally, the chameleon is sensitive to ultraviolet light, allowing it to see things that others cannot.

Both species navigate environments that are more challenging and unpredictable than those faced by humans. Their survival hinges on the development of agility and adaptability.

Much like these two species, the modern executive has to be agile and adaptive. While survival may be possible without these attributes, achieving success is not.

Just like other leadership qualities, enhancing agility and adaptability requires a mindset shift. This involves developing a perspective that embraces and even welcomes change, as well as recognising that risk-taking is nature's way of fostering discovery. It is essential to cultivate heightened awareness that allows you to perceive environmental and situational factors before others do and to blend into new circumstances with minimal effort. Finally, when the decision is made to move forward, you should act swiftly and stay focused on the goal without distractions.

One in every five executives I have coached for leadership development in recent years could benefit from improving their agility and adaptability. Can they achieve this? Most often, yes. In many ways, these qualities represent the natural state of humanity; they may just be clouded by limiting beliefs, fears stemming from past experiences, or a general apprehension about change.

Are they able to grow in these areas? Absolutely. Once the clouds clear, it becomes easier to reach a more natural state of being. With mindfulness and practice, agility and adaptability can be improved.

Talk the Walk

Doing great work is no longer enough; people need to be aware of it. Many professionals hesitate to talk about their achievements, but 'talking your walk' with grace, clarity, and sincerity is a valuable skill to master. This article offers strategies for self-promotion without arrogance, helping you become more visible and valued.

We often hear the phrase "walk the talk". But what about "talking your walk"? A significant portion of senior executives I have coached do not communicate their achievements, capabilities, or ambitions. They believe their work should speak for itself or that others should figure them out on their own and offer growth opportunities accordingly.

Unfortunately, this often doesn't happen. In today's noisy environment—both externally and internally—people are bombarded with information. A thousand words can be spoken in just 7 to 8 minutes. Imagine how many words a person hears in a single day along with everything they read. As a result, the ability to notice you is limited, especially among stakeholders like your managers, peers, team members, and clients. Consider this: how much do you really know about your colleagues? They likely know as much about you!

"I have been working hard, delivering results, and my clients are happy with me, but my manager and his boss do not know it. I don't want to brag," one very senior executive told me.

"I do all the work, but the other guy gets the promotion. I just do not get noticed," says another.

These statements reflect a common issue: doing good work and getting noticed are not the same. If you want your efforts, achievements, and results to be recognised, you must communicate them effectively.

Today, unlike in the past, self-promotion isn't just important—it's critical for success. You must talk your walk. You might fear that sharing your successes will alienate people, but that is unlikely. You risk alienation only if you come across as egotistical or if you put others down, not if you share your accomplishments with genuine pride and pleasure.

So, how do you take the first steps? Here are ten suggestions:

1. "I wanted to share some good news..."
2. Include in informal conversations: "By the way, just to bring you on the same page – we have ..."
3. "You have been a great support to us, so I should let you know that ..."
4. "I just wanted to let you know the team has done a tremendous job –your acknowledgement could be a great encouragement. We completed the job ahead of schedule and saved nearly 5 % in costs.
5. "In addition to the data I'm sending you, I wanted to share that the client is happy and considering a renewal."
6. "Since you have been an integral part of our journey, I thought I would share some good news with you. We recently set a record for ....and it was a very fulfilling experience."
7. Create opportunities to share at formal meetings or town halls. Consider having a happy hour where people share their successes. Encourage your team, collaborators, and clients to share their accomplishments as well.
8. "I have some tremendous news for you! We have expanded our service offerings—at virtually no extra cost."
9. "Recently, we received some great referrals. I am attaching them for your information."
10. Utilise symbolism. For example, I recall receiving a beautifully wrapped package 30 years ago. Inside were two small items, accompanied by a simple message: "We doubled our revenue last year—would like to share our joy with you."

Create your own sound bites and practice them. Sometimes they will come to you naturally, and other times you may need to put in some effort, but either way, they are worth it.

Telling the story and sharing the lessons learned is often the most important part. For example, you might say: "The past few weeks have been eventful—we faced many changes in requirements, supply chain disruptions, medical emergencies, and even an unexpected storm. This taught us that there is no such thing as being fully prepared. We learned that, in uncertain times, creativity and resilience are our best assets. I'm proud that we were able to harness these qualities and navigate this challenging period successfully."

Share your achievements with pride, not ego. Share with modesty, not bravado. This often comes down to tone rather than language. Focus not only on what you say but how you say it. You may not want to blow your trumpet, but how about playing the flute—gently and pleasantly?

River, Dam and Leadership

Some leaders flow like rivers—dynamic, creative, and ever-evolving. Others contain power like dams—steady, structured, and capable of storing strength. This poetic reflection contrasts two powerful leadership archetypes, urging you to understand your dominant style and explore your ability to shift between both when the moment calls for it.

Deep in the mountains, the stream roars down steep gradients. It is loud, frothy, and full of energy. Sometimes it merges with other rivers, and at other times, others merge with it. From its starting point, it finds its own path. If there are obstacles, it goes around them or wears them down. Even today, it occasionally changes course. It exists in a state of ceaseless motion, appearing beautiful and sublime at times, and raging and angry at others. It provides sustenance and livelihood to many—humans and animals alike. It is natural, a force of nature: raw, untamed, and unstoppable.

Then, there is the dam. Behind the dam, the water is still and deep. It allows flow through carefully controlled gates, with turbines that produce electricity for millions of people. The dam controls flow into canals that irrigate thousands of acres of land. It stores energy in vast quantities, releasing it in a controlled, planned manner. It protects the land from flooding and serves as a reserve in times of short supply. Most of the time, it has a serene, calm appearance. Life flourishes in its depths and on its surface. The dam is often man-made, a creation that harnesses the power of nature meaningfully.

I see two different leadership styles reflected in the river and the dam. There are leaders I work with who resemble the river, and others who resemble the dam. Both are related but distinct. The river represents the entrepreneur—the original, the start-up—a bundle of raw energy. The dam represents the assimilator, the channeliser, the manager, and the storehouse of experience and wisdom—the one who provides stability.

Is one style better than the other? A great leader can adapt to both styles, sometimes being the flowing river and other times the steadfast storehouse, depending on the demands of the moment.

What is your style? Can you adapt as needed?

Building Presence: Mindspace or Timespace?

Leadership presence isn't about having more time; it's about consciously using the mind space. This article reframes presence, not as an extra activity but as an embedded practice. It's built through daily interactions, posture, tone, intent, and authenticity—not merely through time spent networking or speaking up.

"I want to build a presence within the organisation, but I do not have time to do so." Variations of this statement frequently arise during the executive coaching sessions I conduct. This implies that building presence is a kind of extra activity for which time must be available. However, there is a fundamental flaw in this statement.

Presence is how you are perceived by others around you. It might be described as cheerful, strong, influential, thoughtful, or various other descriptors. More specifically, executives desire to cultivate leadership presence, which has its own variants. This presence is the ability to connect with and inspire people. It is about being seen with respect, building teams, gaining authority without formal power, and influencing others to accept your ideas or visions.

So, here's a question: If you had an extra hour each day, what would you do to develop your presence? Some might answer, "I will read about it, increase my visibility, network more, or meet with my team," etc. My submission is this: If you do all these things but present yourself in the same way as you currently do, it will not build your presence.

Presence is a style, not an activity you can undertake at specific times. It should always be cultivated in every interaction: listening with intent, being present and mindful of others, practising magnanimity, speaking purposefully, being assertive, being open and friendly, modulating your speaking style, changing body posture, dressing differently, and maintaining a positive and courageous outlook—even during difficult conversations. The list goes on. These are enablers that build leadership presence and are not 'extra' actions that consume time each day. You can perform the same actions but with a different style to cultivate your leadership presence.

This requires being conscious of your own actions as much as possible and remaining present to yourself, even amid distractions. Leadership presence can be cultivated anywhere—at work, at home, at play, or while travelling.

The degree to which you practise this, the sincerity with which you engage it, and the skills you build will determine the extent of your leadership presence. This can take time—weeks, months, or even years.

Thus, while building presence can take time, it does not require dedicated time each day. It needs more mind space than time space.

Tyranny of Tools

While personality tools can be helpful, their overuse or misinterpretation can lead to misleading conclusions. This article cautions against turning assessments into fixed identities and shares coaching insights on using tools as starting points, rather than definitive judgements. True self-awareness, it reminds us, requires more than just a report.

As a practising coach, I often encounter requests for personality tools from clients, their organisations, and even from myself. Over time, I have realised that these tools can become tyrants if not managed well.

There was a young lady I worked with who underwent a 360-degree feedback assessment as part of a leadership development initiative. A twelve-page report detailing the results was sent to her. Like most people, she was very curious to know what others thought of her, but the results were not what she expected.

She questioned the data:

- She tried to correlate the data with the names of the respondents and found faults in their feedback.
- She meticulously examined each subjective comment provided.
- She marked contradictions in the data, whether real or implied.
- She bombarded HR with questions about the methodology used.

Her reaction was extreme and disproportionate. She lost some confidence in herself, and as her coach, I found it difficult to convince her that the report was merely an indicator—one that should kickstart a process of self-awareness and introspection. She wanted a report as precise as a thermometer or a blood pressure reading. For her, the tool had become a tyrant.

I have had similar experiences with other assessment tools as well. All tools and assessments are meant to serve as indicators; human beings are too complex to be defined down to the last detail. We know this, and clients typically understand it, too. However, there are times when they treat these results as gospel and restrict themselves to narrow definitions. I have seen clients come to believe they are not good enough – simply because a test said so—leading to self-fulfilling prophecies.

Another danger is that tools can be taken as the quick route to self-discovery. Clients (and others) often find it easier to be 'told' about their competencies, strengths, desires, improvement areas, behaviours, attitudes, or anything else that the tool 'measures'. In contrast, true introspection and self-discovery is a more intricate and time-consuming process.

My ground rules when discussing the results are:

- Set expectations clearly before the results are shared or discussed.
- Provide sample reports when possible and have a conversation about varied interpretations. It is easier to be objective when someone else is being discussed!
- Try to use the results after the first couple of sessions, ensuring some degree of introspection and trust-building has taken place.
- In a few cases, I have experimented with sharing the executive summary of the report first rather than the detailed findings.

Remember that tools can become tyrants who seek to control your mind and behaviour. You have to keep them at their right place if they have to be useful.

Drowning in Self- Expectations?

High achievers often carry a paradox: external success paired with internal insecurity. This reflective article explores how unrealistic self-expectations can erode confidence, joy, and resilience. It encourages a recalibration—suggesting breaking big goals into achievable steps and pausing to celebrate success rather than continuously sprinting past it.

Managing your expectations from yourself can be challenging. If you don't set any expectations from yourself, you may end up achieving little. Conversely, if your expectations are too high, you might feel overwhelmed.

In my 15-plus years of coaching, I have encountered many high achievers who set lofty expectations for themselves and often meet them. One might expect them to be brimming with self-confidence, pride, and happiness regarding their success. Paradoxically, many of them struggle with low self-esteem, doubt their own capabilities, and generally feel insecure.

What causes this phenomenon?

The answer lies in the way they handle their achievements or setbacks. They are excellent at achieving their goals but struggle to manage that success—or the occasional failure. Upon reaching their goals, they often quickly shift the goalpost, frequently without realising it. They do not take the time to appreciate or acknowledge their successes; instead, they continually seek more, instantly. They are perfectionists, and the relentless pursuit of the next level of perfection leaves them feeling perpetually dissatisfied with themselves. Over time, this dissatisfaction leads to self-doubt.

In some cases, high achievers may set goals that are so distant they are unattainable. While this can be acceptable, frequent self-criticism can lead to diminished self-confidence and low self-esteem, or even an increased fear of failure.

Are you experiencing this? Here are some pointers that may help:

- Do you constantly feel dissatisfied because you believe you can accomplish more?

- Do you often feel that others let you down?
- Are you unable to reflect on your achievements with pride and a smile?
- Are you obsessive about minor details?
- Do you often dwell on what could go wrong?

Does this mean that you should avoid setting goals or have zero expectations from yourself? Absolutely not. However, setting graded expectations may be a better approach for managing your self-expectations.

Set expectations that are slightly out of reach within a specific timeframe—whether it's a quarter, a year, or a couple of years. If you have a substantial goal, break it down into smaller, manageable steps.

Before you begin, take the time to ensure that your expectations are truly your own. Consider what you genuinely want from yourself, rather than what others expect from you or what you might do to please them

When you achieve a goal, take a moment to pause and acknowledge your accomplishment. Enjoy the feeling of success, give yourself a pat on the back, and share your achievement with others. Celebrate your journey by recalling where you started and what you have overcome. Reflect on the lessons you've learned along the way and express gratitude to those who have supported you. Take time to appreciate your blessings and remember to do this more than once.

Once you've fully enjoyed this pause, reset your expectations for the next level, continuing the practice of setting goals that are just a bit more challenging than what comes easily.

If you occasionally miss your goals, be kind to yourself. Avoid blaming the system, becoming a victim, or wallowing in self-pity. Don't turn excuses into reasons. Instead, scale back your expectations for the time being and keep moving forward.

Remember, you cannot leap to the top of a tall building in one go. But you can reach it by taking small steps and using a few benches along the way.

Master of Expectation Management

Expectations—whether from boards, teams, or communities—rarely manage themselves. This powerful coaching case study explores how one executive learned to define, negotiate, and communicate expectations effectively. The takeaway: managing expectations is less about saying yes and more about conversations, empathy, boundaries, and clarity.

A couple of years ago, I was coaching a very senior executive in an organisation. His challenge was to manage the expectations of those around him—expectations that often seemed unrealistic and distant. As the CEO of an industrial plant in a rural area, he was accountable to the board but also responsible to many others. The board wanted growth and a trouble-free environment. The staff needed facilities and support for working in a challenging terrain. The locals expected land to be protected, compensations to be paid, pollution to be managed, and overall, wanted the company to solve all their problems. The local politicians sought contracts for the favoured few and other advantages from the company. The list went on.

We began discussing how expectations are set up. Why are they necessary? And when not met, what havoc do they cause? Are there ways to manage them more effectively?

The initial discussions unfolded somewhat like this:

- Expectations should be ignored if they are unrealistic. Unrealistic for whom?
- If you ignore them, they will go away over time. Do they really go?
- Don't feed them; they'll just become hungrier. But don't they grow stronger if left unfed?

These may not have been his exact words, but they certainly reflected his thoughts.

As he delved deeper, he realised that this mindset was too narrow and rigid. Being a determined individual, he set out to become the "Master of Expectation Management"—his words! While this is not a degree offered by universities, it is certainly a valuable skill.

By the end of our formal engagement, he felt much less stressed, more in control, and his various stakeholders were happier. This was so because even when he could not meet all expectations, he was consciously managing them.

Here are some of his conclusions:

- Having expectations is natural and useful; it drives ambition and growth. The challenge lies in managing the emotions, reactions, stress, and anger related to unmet or even met expectations.
- Understanding stated or unstated expectations is not easy. They are not always articulated clearly, and sometimes people don't know how to express them. There is often a lot of imaginary baggage tied to expectations. But expectations are expectations - real or perceived.
- Initially, he was blaming others—his seniors, staff, and others—for having "unrealistic" expectations of him. However, he realised that no discussions had taken place about what constituted "realistic" or "unrealistic" expectations, and why. No one had initiated that critical conversation. As the CEO, it was his responsibility to do so.
- These conversations were not easy, as they required him to say, "I cannot do this" or "I cannot deliver on some expectations." His ingrained sense of responsibility and desire not to disappoint people often got in the way, as did his ego, which whispered, "What will they think of you?"
- He concluded that expectations are rooted in feelings, and to address those feelings, empathy is often the necessary salve. Data and logic alone were not sufficient when he needed to decline certain expectations. He

discovered that when rational thought failed him, he had little to rely on.

- He also started to believe that setting expectations is a skill that can be learned. It involves clear thinking and improved communication from the outset. Addressing issues early can prevent them from escalating. Under-committing and over-delivering proved to be an effective strategy for managing expectations. Establishing boundaries and clearly defining outcomes is highly beneficial.
- During discussions about expectations, it's acceptable to say no or a conditional yes. You don't need to agree all the time.
- If circumstances change and original expectations regarding schedules, quality, costs, or other business parameters are likely to vary, it's better to communicate this sooner rather than later.
- Individual expectations are often framed as demands in the interest of the organisation and can be presented as urgent when they are not necessarily important or urgent. Asking clarifying questions is an effective way to set and manage expectations: Why is this important? What will happen if we do not do it? What else will be impacted?
- Everyone has biases and preconceptions that influence their expectations. Knowing people and understanding their beliefs can help manage expectations.
- Ultimately, you do not manage expectations; you manage the fears, frustrations, anger, concerns, and insecurities of people.

I believe that the last insight was the most powerful one for him.

Mirror, Mirror, on the Wall

This article explores how the metaphor of the mirror reflects our evolving self-awareness. It emphasises the importance of honest reflection, personal responsibility, and the gap between how we see ourselves and how others perceive us, encouraging alignment between self-image and reality for stronger leadership and personal development.

A key component of self-development is self-reflection, often referred to as "looking in the mirror". Many would argue that this is the single most important key to growth. However, it's essential to consider your mindset while looking in the mirror. We need to approach this reflection positively, much like we should aim for the "good cholesterol" in our lives, not the bad.

So, is your mirror evaluative or judgemental?

Below are some genuine statements from my clients. They are accurate, but not very useful, as they carry judgements that are negative and not action-oriented:

- I am not good at networking and talking to people.
- I struggle to manage my time better. I just cannot prioritise.
- I wish I could speak better; I do not have the vocabulary.
- I am very bad at structuring my thoughts.
- Long- term thinking is not my strength – I can only manage operational roles.
- I don't think I can be tough with my team; it has always been my weakness.
- I somehow get lost in important meetings. I have nothing to say and feel like an outsider.
- People keep telling me to be more proactive. It does not work for me – I have given up.

These can be rephrased to be more evaluative, neutral, factual, and action-oriented, as given below:

- Building a network is important for me. It may not be my intrinsic strength, but I can work on it.
- I tend to get overwhelmed when I have too many tasks in front of me; however, I manage well with just a few. How can I train myself to handle more tasks simultaneously?

- I occasionally struggle to find the right words. Is this truly a limitation? If so, how can I overcome it?
- I have many ideas that come to me at once. Compartmentalising them would benefit me greatly. What skills can I learn to achieve this?
- I excel at managing operations; now I need to explore how I can become more strategic.
- I realise that some situations require a tough approach with my team for their benefit. I must learn from my manager how to adopt this approach.
- I wonder how others make themselves visible in important meetings. This is a skill I have never consciously developed. Where can I find more information about this?
- People give me feedback that I am not proactive. Maybe it is time for me to take initiative in being proactive.

Our thoughts communicate with us, and "thought-speech" is more powerful than we give it credit for. It can undermine our confidence and pull us down or provide options and lift us up.

So, do you judge yourself or evaluate yourself? Do you recognise the subtle but significant difference between the two? If you find yourself judging, can you shift away from that mindset?

Let Go – But of What?

Letting go is a powerful mantra, but what exactly do we release? This article distinguishes between letting go of control, ego, perfectionism, or past hurts, as opposed to simply stopping random actions. It offers clarity to a frequently repeated phrase and encourages conscious detachment from unhelpful patterns rather than fromour core values or purpose.

Most of us have heard the phrase "let go", but what does it truly mean? Often, this idea of letting go is related to actions—things that we do. It might mean letting go of micromanaging tasks, excessive planning, providing unsolicited feedback, overanalysing situations, juggling multiple responsibilities, or distancing ourselves from people who don't align with our goals.

Letting go implies the removal of a burden, which should ideally be a beneficial process that occurs with ease. However, this is often not the case because behind our actions lie underlying mindsets, values, and beliefs. Letting go of actions without addressing these core beliefs is like trying to enter water while holding on to something for comfort; it simply does not work.

It can be helpful to view actions as symptoms of deeper issues. If we change our mindset, our actions will naturally follow suit. Beliefs and mindsets are like loyal friends, not easily cast aside. We must gradually wean ourselves away from them.

What are your enduring beliefs? What reframing might work for you?

Here are a few mindsets shared by people I have coached, along with potential reframing strategies:

Action to be changed	Possible Underlying Belief / Value	Reframed Thought
Micro Management	It saves time if I do things myself.	In the long run, things are completed faster when everyone contributes; given a chance, others can learn.

Action to be changed	Possible Underlying Belief / Value	Reframed Thought
	People are not trustworthy.	Most people can be trusted; someone once trusted me.
	It is my responsibility; I should do it all.	I can be responsible for getting tasks done, but I don't have to do all of them myself.
Overthinking/ Postponing	The best solutions take time.	The best solutions require clarity more than time.
	Risks should be avoided.	Risks should be calculated.
Avoiding Conflict	Relationships are key.	Keys are meant to unlock opportunities, not strengthen barriers.
	People don't change; it is not worthwhile to argue.	It's worthwhile to try, rather than give up without effort.
Not Sharing Successes	"Don't boast" is my motto.	Success can be shared without being boastful. While ego may be detrimental, self-esteem is beneficial.
Work Overload	Saying 'no' will make others dislike me.	If I say 'yes' and fail to deliver, how will that be perceived?
	Challenges bring out the best in me.	Challenges can be beneficial, but constantly living on the edge is not sustainable.

Action to be changed	Possible Underlying Belief / Value	Reframed Thought
Being a Perfectionist	Being perfect is a virtue.	Striving for perfection is admirable, but waiting for it is not.
	Being less than perfect harms my reputation.	Reputation is built on multiple factors, not just one.
Not Speaking Up	This is not my place to speak.	I am here because I belong.
	I may antagonize others.	I can learn to express my thoughts without creating conflict.

Resume Plus

This piece challenges the conventional view of a resume as merely a historical list. Instead, it advocates a strengths-based, future-focused profile that showcases value-adding capabilities. Aimed at mid-to-senior professionals, it shares practical tips to ensure your professional narrative clearly aligns with employer needs and the evolving talent landscape.

One of my earliest coaching assignments was when a well-known multinational corporation decided to shut down operations in India, nearly a decade ago. The lessons from that experience remain relevant to this day.

The shutdown was executed rather secretly. One fine morning, representatives arrived from Hong Kong to announce that operations—and jobs—were being terminated. I was called in to provide career coaching to both young and veteran employees being laid off. I found the assignment quite challenging, and I can only imagine how disturbing it was for those affected.

There was a young lady from one of India's north-eastern states who had just travelled across the country to Gurgaon for this job. Additionally, there was a veteran with over twenty years of service who struggled to find the words to explain the situation to his family—and many others in between.

As I spoke to them, I tried to provide as much emotional support as I could. A line from Allama Iqbal kept resonating in my mind: "*Sitaron Ke Aage Jahan Aur Bhi Hain*," which can be loosely translated to mean that there are worlds beyond the stars. (For more on this, you can check academic translations and a beautiful musical rendition by the incomparable Rahat Fateh Ali Khan.).

I repeated this sentiment to all of them, hoping it provided some encouragement.

Beyond the emotional aspect, practical plans had to be made, and actions taken. Life needed to continue. During our discussions, I realised their resumes were limiting them. They were more than what could be captured on a couple of sheets of paper. Their resumes focused primarily on what they had done—education, jobs, etc. But when we explored the "what next" question, we found that their strengths, achievements, aspirations, values, and motivations were almost entirely absent from their narratives.

Even if they didn't articulate it, they were far more than just their resumes. They needed to believe in their fuller identity to overcome the challenges they faced and be able to communicate that with passion and confidence.

I devised a rough structure to help them position themselves more effectively. They were given 30 minutes to create this. We iterated on it as many times as we could.

The structure included the following:

1. Describe who you are without mentioning your education or job history. (50 words)
2. List your top ten strengths and what you have achieved using these strengths. (100 words)
3. What is unique about you? What do you possess that many others do not? (50 words)
4. If you were applying to an organisation today, what value would you bring to their table? (50 words)

For many, it was challenging to answer these questions—not because they didn't know, but because they had never thought of themselves beyond their resumes. It was even harder to stay within the word limits we set to keep the responses concise and focused.

Some participants later told me that this exercise helped them significantly.

Resume creation has evolved considerably since then, with professional resume writers, books, articles, blogs, and even AI tools. However, in my occasional career coaching sessions now,

I still find that the essence of those questions remains relevant. While the standard of resumes has improved, the ability to effectively position oneself has not necessarily increased. Many still believe that their work speaks for itself, but in today's competitive landscape, that is simply not enough. Others express reluctance, fearing they might come off as boastful. However, there is a significant difference between being egotistical and taking pride in one's accomplishments.

These questions are important not only for resumes and interviews but also for self-awareness, which is as crucial as securing another job.

Power of Acceptance

Acceptance is not resignation; it is a conscious leadership strength. This article examines how embracing reality, rather than resisting it, allows for constructive action. It shifts the mindset from "why me?" to "what now?", creating space for resilience, calm problem-solving, and a powerful presence during uncertainty or failure.

In my coaching conversations, the concept of acceptance often arises, and frequently, there is resistance to the notion. People question why they should accept difficult situations. Many equate acceptance with weakness, viewing it as capitulating to circumstances or demands, failing to stand up to things they consider wrong, or failing to stand up for what they believe is right.

Why is this perception so prevalent?

For some, acceptance feels like a loss of control or an admission of defeat, which can hurt their self-esteem. For others, there is a bias against acceptance because society often elevates nonconformists to the status of heroes. Additionally, many mistake acceptances for passivity, believing that it means relinquishing all attempts to improve the situation.

Consider the case of a CEO of an organisation I work with. He has been put in charge of a poorly performing unit that faces significant political interference and has an ingrained culture of low involvement and low productivity. There is limited room for growth, and he is close to retirement. Given his successful tenure with the organisation, he was assigned to this troubled unit because he wanted to leave on a high note.

In our initial sessions, our discussions focused on how past leaders had mismanaged the unit. There were complaints about a lack of support for change, a pervasive laziness among employees, incessant demands from politicians for favours, and the powerful influence of the workers' union. Unlike his previous roles, where he received support from the top, this time there was none. His focus remained on the past—a past that could not be changed.

At the end of one such session, I suggested that he needed to accept the reality of the situation. He seemed aggrieved and questioned whether he should simply bide his time until retirement.

I encouraged him to pause and evaluate what non-acceptance of reality was doing for him. The conclusion we reached was that it was not yielding any positive outcomes. If that were true, why continue down that path?

He then chose to change his approach and move forward. He did not want to retire feeling that he hadn't tried – it would be cheating himself.

Acceptance can be seen as a weakness if it leads to passivity and inaction regarding the situation. However, it can be a powerful tool if it enables you to let go of the past and focus on building a future. The real issue is not the acceptance of reality but the choices that follow. You can either ignore reality and stay stuck in the past or embrace it and move forward. The latter option can be a liberating force.

Acceptance has several other positive effects:

- It can shift you from inaction to action.
- It can reduce the stress and anxiety associated with struggling to change what cannot be altered.
- It can facilitate growth and learning through new opportunities.
- It can help you become less judgemental of yourself and enhance your emotional well-being.
- It can improve your relationships.
- It fosters resilience, enabling you to bounce back and move on.

The CEO is now actively engaging with the challenges at hand, recognising that his efforts may not yield immediate results during his tenure. He understands that the journey may be rocky and risky, but he believes it is still worthwhile.

What path would you choose if you were in a similar position in some aspect of your life?

Grow the Box

We often hear the phrase "think outside the box", but what if we focused on growing the box instead? This article suggests expanding our capabilities and frameworks from within existing systems. It reframes creative problem-solving as an evolutionary process — encouraging adaptive leadership that scales responsibly from within.

Creativity is frequently associated with the idea of thinking outside the box in organisations. The Cambridge Dictionary defines creativity as the "ability to produce or use original and unusual ideas", while it describes an organisation as "a group of people who work together in an organised way for a shared purpose". This "organised way" is shaped by rules, processes, norms, and other boundaries, which can often be viewed as inhibitors of creativity

Managers are expected to be creative and foster creativity& have the ability to think out of the box while simultaneously operating within the constraints of their organisations. This like being inside and outside the box.

So what is the alternative? By harnessing creativity within the established framework, organisations can promote innovation without losing structure. This may seem contradictory since creativity is often considered spontaneous and free. However, my experience shows that creativity can be fostered and harnessed effectively. It is the manager's role to encourage this in themselves and in their teams.

Be Curious

Encourage yourself and your team to be curious—ask questions and become more aware of the environment in which your business operates. Rudyard Kipling once said:

> "I keep six honest serving-men
> (They taught me all I knew);
> Their names are What and Why and When
> And How and Where and Who."

These fundamental questions still hold value today. Questions based on these six prompts enable curiosity, expand the mind, and foster new ideas. Consider the following: How else can this be accomplished? What are the enablers? Where is the problem localised? Who can perform this task better? When will this impact my business? How is the competition addressing it? What avenues have we yet to explore? And more.

Capture Ideas

Generating ideas alone is not enough, even if they are original and unusual. According to Dr Deepak Chopra, an average human being has 50,000 to 60,000 thoughts a day, many of which are unusual or relate to your business. However, ideas need to be captured because they have a high mortality rate; they come and go like shooting stars. If you don't capture them in some way for future use, they are likely to be forgotten. Use notepads, messages to yourself, reminders—whatever works. Don't rely on your memory to retain all your generated ideas; it doesn't work that way. Recognise when and where your mind is most active and filled with new thoughts. This could be during a flight, while taking a walk, or just before bed. Develop a method for capturing ideas when they arise. And capture them for later evaluation and execution.

Make Connections

Once ideas are captured, they must be connected to your business. Joining the dots is important. For example, a product manager in a telecom company reads about AI and its potential for changing the way we work. He captures the idea by sending himself a message. Later, he reflects on its impact on his work, connecting it to demand forecasting and other future changes. This connection wouldn't have happened if the idea hadn't been captured and associated with his work.

Build Confidence

Next comes the confidence needed to express these ideas to others and to take chances on new approaches. Self-confidence and a supportive environment that encourages creative thinking without judgement are crucial. In short-term, target-driven environments, innovative ideas often get overlooked. Good managers foster a supportive environment by building confidence in themselves and others to speak up, share, and experiment with ideas without the fear of judgement.

Create Challenges

Setting challenges can also reveal untapped potential. For example, I worked with a senior consultant who aimed to increase her profit centre's revenue by 25% in the next year. She thought this was a good target given the organisation's growth of about 15%. Out of curiosity, I asked her why it couldn't be 35% or only 10% with a higher margin. Her mindset had simply not considered these possibilities—this is common for many of us. We push beyond the obvious only when challenged.

Later, she told me that my question had profoundly impacted her. She challenged herself and her team with it, resulting in a remarkable 36.8% growth the following year. They dropped some old clients and brought in new, high-growth ones—an idea they hadn't previously explored due to the comfort of established relationships. Challenge serves as a powerful catalyst for sparking creativity.

In conclusion, it is indeed possible to harness creativity by fostering an environment of curiosity, capturing ideas, making connections, building confidence, and creating challenges. This approach enables growth while remaining within the box.

Confidence Plus

The space you occupy belongs to you. Confidence is more than charisma. This article unpacks the deeper roots of authentic confidence—awareness, preparation, and purpose—and its quiet power in leadership. It shows how true confidence encompasses vulnerability, values, and self-assurance rather than mere showmanship or volume.

Many years ago (1982 – 1985), I led the computer department of a large organisation during its early years of computer adaptation. Naturally, there was significant resistance, particularly from senior managers. As I was just starting my career and was among the few who had actually worked with computers and could write code, I was the specialist. I found myself in a challenging position. Many senior colleagues lacked time for the reports generated by our team, leading to the mortifying experience of seeing them sitting idle on desks before being discarded. I felt inadequate and even useless as a result.

I repeatedly complained to my manager, who was supportive and fast-tracked my promotion so that I could attend the monthly senior managers' meetings. He suggested I use these opportunities to influence them about the work we were doing.

I found myself placed in a large conference room with a very big table, alongside the company founder, managing director, board members, and other senior managers.

While I attended a few of these meetings, I didn't say much. I felt anxious beforehand, running through everything I planned to say in my mind. I promised myself that I would speak up when it mattered, but those moments were rare. Instead, I sat in judgement, convincing myself that these conservative people wouldn't understand or appreciate the benefits of computerisation.

The reality was that I felt very uncomfortable. I worried about making a fool of myself, having my ideas rejected, being laughed at, my reports being inaccurate, or what others would think of me. Speaking in front of more experienced people, even if their expertise wasn't related to my work, added to my discomfort. Eventually, I quit after a few months.

Much later, I realised that I was suffering from authority anxiety; I simply lacked the confidence to engage fully. Instead of building my confidence in that situation, I chose to move on. However, true confidence does not come from avoiding challenges—it comes from confronting and overcoming them. This realisation helped me greatly. When faced with new, uncomfortable situations, I began to stick it out, developing resilience and the ability to influence others with my ideas. Overall, this approach worked out well for me.

I often see accomplished managers feeling overwhelmed in the presence of their seniors or in other uncomfortable situations. I have been there myself. Many achievers or specialists are given opportunities to engage with senior leaders because they are talented and have potential—others see it, but they often do not.

What goes wrong? Why do articulate individuals get tongue-tied? Why do people who have the potential to be leaders feel like imposters? This is so because they forget that they are at the table for a reason. They have been invited there; they did not invite themselves. Their presence is not an accident.

Do you feel this way in certain situations? If so, ask yourself why you were invited. It is because someone believes you have a role to play, that you can contribute, and that your work is important to the organisation and the people at the table. They sense you have the potential to be part of the senior club.

Of course, they expect you to prove yourself—demonstrate that you have what it takes to be at the big table. However, you won't prove yourself by remaining silent and trying to blend in.

Yet, I have many clients who do precisely that. They have everything except confidence. They suffer from authority anxiety and /or imposter syndrome—two related psychological challenges that have a similar impact.

Authority Anxiety

This refers to the fear or discomfort experienced when interacting with or being evaluated by individuals in positions of authority, such as supervisors, managers, or other figures of power.

Key Characteristics:

1. Fear of Judgement: Worrying about being judged, criticised, or rejected by those in authority.
2. Power Dynamics: Often stems from perceived power imbalances in professional or personal settings.
3. Impact on Behaviour: Avoidance of authority figures, excessive caution, or overly submissive behaviour.

Common Symptoms:

1. Nervousness or stress during interactions with authority figures.
2. Hesitation to express opinions or make decisions in their presence.
3. Difficulty accepting feedback or constructive criticism.

Imposter Syndrome

This involves feelings of self-doubt and a pervasive fear of being exposed as a fraud, despite evidence of competence and success.

Key Characteristics:

1. Self-Doubt: A lack of belief in one's own abilities, often despite objective accomplishments.

2. Fear of Exposure: Anxiety about being "found out" as inadequate or unqualified, even when there is no concrete evidence to support these feelings.
3. Attribution of Success: A tendency to attribute achievements to luck or external factors rather than personal competence.

Common Symptoms:

1. Persistent feelings of inadequacy despite success.
2. Belief that one's achievements are not deserved or that others will eventually discover their "true" incompetence.
3. Overworking or perfectionism to compensate for perceived inadequacies.

Comparison

Focus: Authority anxiety is specifically about interactions with and evaluations by those in power, while imposter syndrome relates to internal doubts and fears regarding one's own abilities.

Root Causes: Authority anxiety is often rooted in external power dynamics and fear of judgement, whereas imposter syndrome stems from internalised self-doubt and insecurity.

Symptoms: Authority anxiety manifests as nervousness or avoidance around authority figures, while imposter syndrome involves feelings of fraudulence and inadequacy, often in the context of personal achievements and competence.

Bottomline

Either way, the key antidote to anxiety is building confidence. Engaging with senior individuals can be challenging, but with the right strategies, you can feel more at ease and significantly reduce your anxiety.

Here are several ideas to help you get started. Often, just taking the first step is all you need to gain momentum. You don't have to implement all these strategies—choose the ones that resonate with you.

1. Prepare Thoroughly: Familiarise yourself thoroughly with your material or topic. Whether you're attending a meeting, giving a presentation, or having a conversation with a superior, practise what you want to say. The more well-prepared you are; the more confidence you will project.
2. Practise Your Communication: Rehearse what you intend to say beforehand. This can help you articulate your thoughts clearly and reduce nervousness. Focus not just on the content but also on how you deliver it. Consider the sequence of your points, the tone of your voice, and your positioning in the room. Good content presented poorly is a missed opportunity.
3. Understand Their Perspective: Remember that senior individuals often have extensive experience. Approach interactions as opportunities to learn from them and show respect for their knowledge. This mindset can make the situation feel less intimidating and encourage openness.
4. Start Small: If possible, begin with smaller interactions or group settings before engaging in one-on-one conversations. This approach can help build your confidence gradually. Set small, achievable goals for interacting with authority figures. Celebrate your successes and challenge yourself with more complex situations as you build confidence.

5. Ask Questions: Showing curiosity and asking thoughtful questions can demonstrate your interest and engage senior individuals in a meaningful way. This approach also relieves some pressure for you to be the sole expert in the discussion.
6. Body Language Matters: Stand tall, maintain eye contact, and smile. Positive body language can enhance your confidence and project it to others.
7. Focus on Common Ground: Identify shared interests or experiences with the senior individual, whether work-related or personal. It can help create a connection and make the interaction feel more comfortable.
8. Accept Imperfection: Recognise that it's okay not to be perfect. Senior individuals typically value genuine engagement and your ideas more than a flawless presentation. Obsessing over potential missteps can heighten anxiety.
9. Build Self-Awareness: Reflect on your strengths and past successes. Reminding yourself of your achievements can boost your self-confidence.
10. Identify the Source of Your Anxiety: Determine where your anxiety originates. Are you fearful of being judged, criticised, or rejected? Understanding the root of your fear can help you address it more effectively.
11. Challenge Negative Thoughts: Often, authority anxiety is fuelled by negative or irrational thoughts. Challenge these thoughts by questioning whether they are based on facts or are exaggerated.
12. Build Your Confidence: Engage in activities that enhance your self-esteem. Acknowledge your achievements, no matter how small, to foster a sense of accomplishment and build confidence.

13. Seek Feedback: Constructive feedback can help you improve and feel more secure. Regularly seek feedback from your superiors in a way that feels comfortable for you. Use it as an opportunity for growth rather than a source of anxiety.
14. Develop Assertiveness Skills: Being assertive means expressing your thoughts and needs openly and respectfully. Practise assertive communication to feel more in control and less anxious.
15. Use Relaxation Techniques: Incorporate techniques like deep breathing, mindfulness, and meditation into your routine to manage anxiety in the moment and reduce overall stress.
16. Seek Support: Talking to a mentor, coach, or therapist can provide you with additional strategies and support. They can offer perspective, advice, and encouragement as you work through your anxiety.
17. Focus on the Relationship: View authority figures as people rather than just figures of power. Building a positive relationship with them can make interactions feel less intimidating.

Overcoming anxiety takes time and practice, so be patient with yourself as you work through these strategies.

Remember, the space you occupy belongs to you.

The Power of the Pause

Pausing isn't inaction; it's a form of leadership intelligence. This article explores the intentional pause as a tool for emotional regulation, better decision-making, and being present. It reminds readers that the most powerful responses often emerge in the stillness between stimulus and reaction.

For many people I work with, the need to become a more effective communicator is a prime requirement. One of the key enablers is using the pause to good effect. Many of my clients find themselves talking "too much". They struggle to identify when to pause or how to make the most of a pause.

What makes it so difficult to pause? Here are some answers I have collated from my clients:

1. I have a lot to say. If I pause, I may not get a chance to speak again.
2. The listener may not have understood me, so I feel the need to explain myself further.
3. I don't notice myself when I am speaking, so I do not know when to pause.
4. I've never considered it before. Is pausing important? What's the benefit?
5. I have a very active mind, and it keeps generating new thoughts to share.
6. In fast-paced conversations, I feel pressured to respond quickly. Taking a pause might cause me to fall behind.
7. Interrupting the conversation flow with pauses feels awkward and disrupts the rhythm.
8. I worry about how silence will be interpreted.
9. There is too much to do. It seems more efficient to keep moving quickly. Pausing might seem like a sign of inefficiency.
10. Decisive people tend to speak quickly.

Notwithstanding these challenges, the pause is a powerful communication tool. It can make communication more impactful and enrich conversations. Sometimes, the most impactful moments come from the pauses rather than from the spoken words. A well-placed pause can lend weight to what's been said, allowing it to resonate more deeply—much like letting echoes settle before continuing. If you dig deeper, you will find that the simple act of pausing can accomplish a great deal.

Pausing provides the other person with time and mental space to reflect. It allows for thoughtful responses, helping to avoid impulsive or disrespectful reactions.

Benefits of pausing include:

1. Increased ability to listen.
2. Introduction of fresh energy and ideas, leading to more considered decisions.
3. Enhanced creativity and clarity of perspective.
4. Conflict resolution by cooling emotional tensions.
5. Demonstration of empathy and understanding.
6. Crisp and meaningful communication.
7. Stress reduction, helping you regain composure.
8. Added thoughtfulness and gravitas to your presence, promoting mindfulness and self-awareness.
9. Greater influence, as your words carry more weight.
10. Creation of impactful communication, which is one of the primary objectives of conversation.

By pausing strategically, an anticipation and focus is created, which can make your subsequent actions or statements more impactful and dynamic. It's akin to winding up before a powerful throw; the pause builds tension and prepares the environment for a more effective delivery. A pause enhances the effectiveness of the action that follows, making it more decisive and deliberate.

A pause can be long or short. It can be introduced with a thoughtful question, seamlessly integrated using a transition sentence, or simply through nodding or brief silence. In any form, it enriches the conversation.

So why is practising the pause so difficult?

The reasons mentioned above are one set and mostly not true. However, they have become entrenched beliefs that we live by, often without recognising the consequences.

There can be a compulsive need to respond or retort—be ready with an answer even before the other person has completed their thought. This can hinder genuine listening.

Sometimes, the urge arises to add a point simply to appear knowledgeable, driven by ego rather than empathy or rationality. Others may feel compelled to prove a point or "win" the conversation, but conversations should be about learning rather than winning or losing; it's arguments that can be won or lost.

Even the TV remote has a PAUSE button. Perhaps you should consider having a pause button for yourself too, as it can significantly add power to your communication.

As Jack Benny, the great American entertainer, once said, "It's not so much knowing when to speak, as when to pause."

Lessons From Rawat Ji

Through a vivid anecdote from his sales days, the author shares a timeless lesson learned from Rawat Ji: customer decisions are rarely just technical—they're social, emotional, and practical. This serves as a vital reminder for professionals to stay attuned not just to processes, but to people.

Rawat Ji never purchased anything from me. He never paid me. Yet, he imparted something invaluable—a profound lesson. Rawat ji was the owner of a small oil mill in Kanpur, India. He was always dressed in a *dhoti* and vest, with a *tilak* on his forehead and a *paan* in his mouth.

Once upon a time, I worked as a salesman selling generating sets. My territory included Kanpur, Agra, and other parts of Uttar Pradesh. At that time, there was a significant power shortage, and every industrial unit needed a genset—not just as a backup, since the electricity board's supply was unreliable. The government offered a 50% subsidy on the purchase of gensets, reimbursing half of the cost, which made the market very attractive. I was given a list of over 100 potential customers to visit and convince to buy our equipment. This often meant travelling by cycle rickshaw in the hot sun to small organisations, equipped with an umbrella and a grey briefcase, either Aristocrat or VIP—I can't recall.

My organisation was small but professional, with many engineers and MBAs dedicated to serving customer needs. Our process involved first collecting customer requirements. Since my customers were typically small oil mills, metal shops, and workshops, they often had no idea about the genset capacity needed. We designed a form for them to fill out, which listed motors or other electrical equipment along with their KVA ratings. However, most people had no idea about KVA, and the specification plates on their equipment had usually worn off. This meant I had to visit their locations, gather equipment details, and measure the current being drawn. These were often dingy factories, filled with the smell of chemicals, oil, and sweat. Occasionally, there would be a cooler in a corner or in the workshop supervisor's room. I would try and get there as quickly as possible to calculate the power requirements from all the data collected. Then I would ask questions about their proposed expansion plans to estimate future needs, which sometimes elicited amused reactions from the customers. After gathering all the information, we would send a formal quotation by post (no email in those times) and await a response. More often than not, there was no reply, as my customers were not the writing types – business was typically conducted over the phone or in person.

In one quarter I had zero sales. I trundled off once again to Kanpur on a morning train from New Delhi. In the afternoon, I arrived at a mustard oil mill, complete with noisy machines, high temperatures, and a pungent smell in the air. I was offered a cold drink, but when I tried to discuss business, there was little enthusiasm.

I pushed on –zero sales were enough incentive to put aside all ego and make a plea for at least a trial order.

"Okay," said Shri Rawat, the owner. "I will give you an order, but you have to do something. "With the misguided confidence of youth, I asked him to name it, and I would ensure he received it. His request was straightforward: "Raise an invoice for double the amount you have quoted and make it for the largest genset you can supply." My brain raced– why was he offering double the amount? And why for the largest genset when his need was clearly smaller?

He quickly clarified, "But I will pay only half the invoice value." I still did not get it. He patiently explained that he would qualify for the 50% subsidy, effectively making the genset free for him. As for the desire for the largest genset, it was not for future expansion but a matter of prestige; he wanted to be seen as the big man in his area. While we were calculating KVA, he was focused on societal status and financial benefit.

I was stumped. This scenario had never been discussed in our strategy meetings. Nevertheless, it was an opening. With a mixture of excitement and urgency, I rushed back to the railway station and took the night train back. The next morning, I shared my experience with the team at the office. Not surprisingly, it was deemed impossible for us to provide inflated invoices—rightfully so. I lost that order. There were other suppliers who managed to find workarounds.

The lesson was clear: balancing organisational needs with customer needs is not easy.

Customer requirements can be more complex than engineering calculations and management thinking, and my organisation and I were not in touch with that complexity. We approached the situation solely from the perspective of our products, processes, and constraints without prioritising the customer. That did not work.

I'm grateful I learned this lesson early in my career. Thank you, Rawat Ji. I share this story often in my coaching conversations.

Twists, Turns and Success

Leadership is like dancing through unexpected rhythms. This article describes how anticipation, adaptability, and agility determine how leaders respond to the inevitable twists and turns in the workplace. With actionable tips and vivid metaphors, it encourages graceful navigation through change—both on the dance floor and in the boardroom.

In the workplace, there are always twists and turns. You must adapt accordingly. If done well, you can dance your way to success.

Every leader or manager experiences this daily—many times over. Schedules change. Agendas shift. People leave. Teams evolve. Client demands fluctuate. Priorities are redefined. Budgets are adjusted. Policies change. Competition varies. Political dynamics shift. These changes come in many forms: small or large, tactical or strategic. The list is extensive.

A key determinant of success is how effectively you manage these twists by executing well-timed turns. This is akin to dancing, where your partner changes steps, the beat of the music alters, or the crowd moves in a different direction. You can't stop or leave the stage; you must keep dancing, preferably with fluid and graceful movements.

Have you ever wondered how to execute these turns more effectively? Here are the three most powerful qualities you need in both dance and the business world:

1. Anticipation

If you can see or feel what is going to happen next, you can respond more effectively. It is like being in the present but with an eye on the future. Can you become better at anticipation? Yes, it's a skill that improves with practice.

Many managers focus entirely on execution, fixated on the immediate present. They want to navigate the "here and now" without consciously attempting to become more aware of the environment, anticipate trends, and connect them to their business. This lack of future-mindedness can lead to an overreliance on experience, which may hinder innovation.

When evaluating ideas solely based on experience, the ability to anticipate future changes becomes compromised.

Here are three ways to strengthen your anticipation skills:

- Keep an eye out for early signs of future trends. They may be vague and untested, but some will turn out to be significant. Stay aware of them.
- Trends on their own are interesting, but they become useful only when you connect them to your business. Make a conscious effort to link these dots.
- Regularly question your own assumptions about the future—more than once. Remember, assumptions are not always valid.

2. Adaptability

Anticipation is not the only essential quality. When the music changes, you need to adapt to the new beat. This requires a willingness to change and the ability to unlearn and relearn. You should let go of the past while still using relevant lessons learned.

A common excuse many managers give for being inflexible is the lack of time. However, being adaptable is not about having more time; it's about having a different mindset. Changing your perspective can happen in an instant. What's needed is courage and a willingness to take risks on a new path.

Here are some ways to enhance your adaptability:

- Be open to change and respond enthusiastically to new plans. The key is to embrace change proactively, rather than only when necessary
- Be receptive to different perspectives and opinions. Accept feedback with an open mind and heart. Many people perceive themselves as open-minded, yet few

truly are. The natural response to new opinions is often defensive, allowing ego to overshadow reason.

- Taking on new challenges can help you become more adaptable. The key idea is to push yourself out of your comfort zone. While the first steps may be challenging, many managers report positive experiences after embracing change, feeling it was not so difficult. This cuts across levels, industries, and type of change. Focus on reasons to move forward rather than reasons to stay stagnant, and then watch the magic unfold.

Resilience is also a crucial trait that supports adaptability. It is often underrated or taken for granted. Not many people consciously work on enhancing their resilience—they tend to give up too soon in the face of challenging conversations and situations.

3. Agility

The final quality in the story of twists and turns is agility. Eventually, everyone changes, but that's not sufficient in the real world. The speed of adaptation is as crucial as the adaptation itself. This is where agility comes into play—the ability to understand, think, and move quickly. Quick movement often requires taking risks and making intuitive decisions, especially when faced with twists that lack historical data or precedent.

This is where the difference between good dancers and great ones becomes evident—in their movements. Some dancers exhibit grace, while others appear laboured and contrived.

An agile manager anticipates, adapts, and moves quickly. They focus on their task rather than looking around to see who is watching. In contrast, a less agile manager relies on past experiences, gathers more data, and takes longer to discuss options, which ultimately results in them falling behind. In a sprint, the distinction between the medal winners and the "also rans" can come down to mere milliseconds, highlighting the importance of who gets off the mark first. The first-mover advantage is irreplaceable.

In my experience, many managers tend to seek comfort in data, often doubting their intuition. Making quick decisions requires confidence and the ability to face the potential consequences. This quality is what distinguishes great managers from good ones.

While you cannot control unexpected twists, you can improve how you manage turns through anticipation, adaptability, and agility—not only on the dance floor but also at the workplace.

The Myth of the Right Decision

We often chase the illusion of the 'right' decision. But what if clarity emerges not before, but after the choice is made? This article explores the myth of perfect decisions and how growth often lies in committing to what you choose, rather than choosing perfectly.

We all make decisions every day and have been doing so for years. By now, it should be an easy task. Yet, in coaching conversations, the concern about making the right decision frequently arises. One reason for this is that there is no such thing as the 'right' decision; it is a myth. Every decision comes with its own pros and cons and an element of uncertainty. Instead of fixating on making the right decision, think about making the best decision. This shift in mindset can help decisions flow more easily.

Under what circumstances is decision-making difficult? Here are some common responses collected from various individuals:

1. When a quick response is needed. In such situations, I tend to delay my decisions. This feedback has also been shared with me.
2. When I lack sufficient data or knowledge.
3. When I must have difficult conversations, such as addressing an employee's performance or terminating someone.
4. When significant consequences are involved, like accepting or rejecting a large order.
5. When there are no corporate guidelines provided, or I have not been informed that I can make certain decisions.
6. When I worry about being questioned regarding my authority.
7. When faced with too many choices and ambiguity.
8. When I am concerned about what others will think of me.
9. When I am apprehensive about potential negative outcomes.
10. When I am tired or under stress.

Here are the top ten factors that impede the decision-making process, along with possible strategies to overcome them:

1. Fear of Failure: You may worry about making the wrong choice and facing negative consequences. Can you begin to view failure as an opportunity for learning and growth?
2. Lack of Information: You might feel you do not have enough information or knowledge to decide. Accept that there will be situations where complete information is unattainable; this can expand your options. Consider reaching out to others for support or trust your intuition and experience, rather than relying solely on data.
3. Feeling Overwhelmed: Are you in a situation with too many options, making it hard to choose? Break it down into smaller steps. Start with simpler actions so you can pivot if necessary. Remember, like walking through a forest, sometimes you just need to start moving to carve your path.
4. Perfectionism: Do you seek a perfect solution, leading to delayed decisions? Look around—are there any perfect decisions? Perfection is a myth and often hinders speed and progress. Focus on making the best decision possible rather than the perfect one.
5. Risk Aversion: If you are hesitant to take risks, do you find yourself delaying decisions until there's no choice left, or until someone else makes them for you? Understand that every decision carries a risk-reward ratio. Are you willing to forgo the potential rewards of money, recognition, growth, and satisfaction simply for safety? The problem often is not the decision but living with its consequences. Good decision-makers can find the right balance between the risk of taking a decision

and that of avoiding one. Often, the risks involved in not taking a decision are greater than those of taking one.

6. External Pressures: You may know what decision is best, but external influences or societal expectations can impact you. While looking good and keeping everyone happy is important, it can lead to indecisiveness. Consider that appearing decisive and confident can also enhance your image. Which path do you prefer?
7. Emotional Factors: Strong emotions such as anxiety, stress, or excitement can cloud judgement. Are they a part of your life currently? If so, take time to manage your emotions first. Allow yourself a pause until you feel calmer before making decisions.
8. Decision Fatigue: If you've made several significant decisions in a short time, you may experience mental exhaustion. Take a brief pause to engage in a different activity before revisiting the decision.
9. Lack of Confidence: Do you often feel uncertain about your ability to make decisions? Thoughts like "I am too new", "I am too junior", or "I have never done this before" can frequently cross your mind. Low self-confidence or self-doubt can hinder your decision-making ability.

Remember, building self-confidence is a process. Confidence aids in decision-making, and the act of making decisions helps build confidence. This creates a classic chicken-and-egg scenario. Instead of overthinking it, take a deep breath and start making decisions. As you continue to make more good decisions, your confidence will naturally grow.

10. Role Boundaries: Do you ever question whether a decision is yours to make? Are you concerned about stepping on anyone's toes?

Consider that there are often grey areas in roles, and overlaps in responsibilities are common. No job boundary is ever completely clear-cut, and that will always be the case. If possible, clarify any uncertainties with the relevant people or your manager. If that's not an option, you can test the waters by taking a decision or two and observing the outcomes. Pushing the boundaries of your role can be effective, and if things don't go as planned, you can always step back and move on.

There is no such thing as a completely right decision. Leaders take the best possible decisions based on a combination of information, data, analysis, experience, and intuition. Additionally, they have the confidence to accept the consequences of their decisions.

Can you cultivate that confidence in yourself and your team?

Making the Decision Right

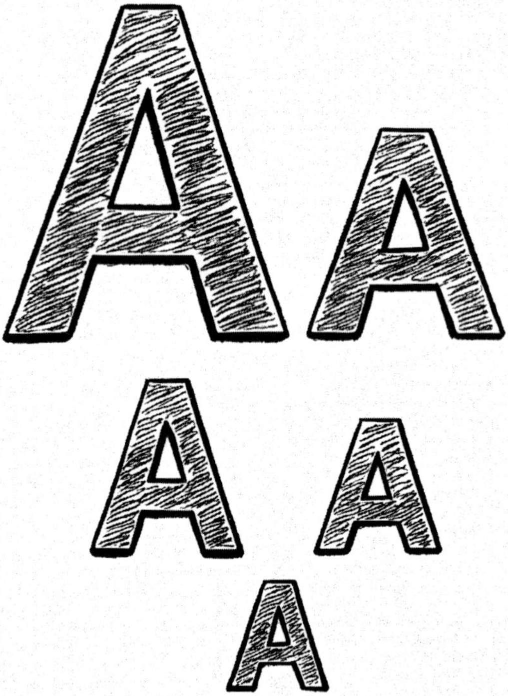

Instead of obsessing over making the right decision, consider focusing on making the decision right. This shift—from anxiety to agency—can transform how we view risk, choice, and responsibility.

Five As for Making the Decision Right

In coaching conversations, one recurring topic is decision-making. Many people express a desire for coaching in this area, often labelling it as their weakness. My usual response is that I am yet to meet anyone who does not take decisions. We are having this conversation because you made the decision to be here. So, could you elaborate on the specific aspects of decision-making that trouble you? This often requires some reflection and exploration.

This leads to multiple ideas about how to take the right decision, which is actually a myth. Are decisions ever completely right or wrong? Have you ever taken a decision where you were one hundred percent sure you were right? Has anyone? All decisions come with their pros and cons. You must decide which pros are desirable for you and which cons you can live with.

What about decisions that do not turn out as expected? These need to be addressed too; otherwise, they can cast long shadows. This calls for a different mindset and skill set, which I refer to as "Making the Decision Right". Even if your decision doesn't meet expectations, this approach allows you to move forward with confidence and speed, avoiding the trap of analysis paralysis.

What can be done to make a decision right? Here are five As that will help:

1. Accept: Recognise that there is no such thing as a completely right decision. Most leaders operate on a best-effort basis, making decisions based on the information available at the time. And that is the way it must be.

2. Adapt: If things don't go according to plan, adapt. Focus on minimising losses and consider what can be done moving forward rather than dwelling on what could have been done in the past. Getting stuck in past decisions can be detrimental.
3. Agility: Move as quickly as possible. The longer you linger in the past, the deeper you sink into the quicksand of self-incrimination. Concentrate on what you've learned rather than engaging in endless "what if" scenarios.
4. Abandon: Be prepared to abandon the old path – partially or completely. You may be sticking to it because your ego is hurt, because you can't admit that you were not perfect, or because you feel the need to prove to others that you were right and they were wrong. You might want to show that your decision was correct while others messed it up. Whatever the reason, the inability to let go of decisions often costs more than the decision itself.
5. Apologise: This is a tough one. It's important to apologise to others who may have been impacted by your decisions. A simple "Sorry, there has been a mess-up" can go a long way. If needed, apologise to yourself, too: "Sorry I messed up." It's okay to make mistakes; what's not okay is staying with the mess.

This does not imply that initial decision- making should be done without due diligence—do that by all means. But remember that living with the consequences of decisions is often tougher than taking the decisions themselves.

The Hard Part of Soft Skills

Soft skills are anything but soft. They require hard work, self-awareness, and emotional strength. This piece breaks down why developing skills such as empathy, communication, and self-regulation is more difficult—and more essential—than it may appear.

Soft skills are key areas of development in many coaching conversations. Executive presence, communication skills, strategic mindset, empathy, handling difficult conversations, and developing gravitas are just a few examples. For several reasons, identifying specific concerns and working on them is not easy.

Here is a summary of a specific conversation with a client from a global consulting firm:

X – Person being coached

C – Coach

X: I have received feedback that my executive presence needs improvement, especially in front of senior stakeholders. My manager says that this is critical for my growth to the next level, and I have opted for coaching to address this.

C: Okay. So this is the feedback you received. How do you perceive your presence when senior stakeholders are present?

X: I don't know. I asked my manager about it but have not got a clear reply. I also spoke to some colleagues who say that I speak very well. I am worried since the performance review is coming up soon, and if I miss this chance, I will have to wait another year.

C: I sense that you feel very concerned about the future right now.

X: Yes. I am a well-qualified technologist and have done excellent work in all my previous assignments. In fact, I was hired for my strong track record. Now, after three years, my growth is at stake, and no one is telling me what to do.

C: Right. You are a technology person. Let's go back to the beginning. What does executive presence mean to you?

X: I think it has something to do with my knowledge and how I come across. It relates to how I speak. However, I have always been a good speaker; I even won debates in college. Some friends suggest this feedback is just an excuse to deny my promotion because the organisation is having a revenue shortfall. They say I should just demand that the promises made at the time of hiring be honoured. They think I am not assertive enough.

C: Do you agree with your friends?

X: I don't think so. I am usually assertive. This situation is different.

C: How would you describe your emotions right now?

X: I think I am angry.

C: What might be a way to move from this anger to something more constructive?

X: I guess I need to increase my presence and convince my manager and others that I am capable.

C: Earlier, you mentioned that to you, presence is how you come across. If you were an observer in the room, how would you describe yourself?

X: (After a pause) I think I would say that I seem a bit tentative. On topics where I have knowledge or have prepared in advance, there is no problem. On others that come up unexpectedly, I do not feel confident enough to speak. If I do speak, it is usually tentative, and I do not create a strong impact. Maybe no one listens to what I am saying.

C: So, the tentativeness arises in areas where you feel less informed. I'm sure everyone in the room has some topics they are not well-informed about. Have you ever wondered how they manage to assert their presence?

X: Hmmm. I guess they can size up the situation quickly and speak accordingly. I've also noticed that they sometimes say, "We can take this offline" or "I don't have the details at this moment." They seem comfortable admitting they don't know everything.

C: That is a very astute observation. Does it suggest a way forward for you?

X: I guess I need to accept that it is fine to not know all the details about every topic.

Finally, a specific issue emerged along with a possible way forward. One option—a starting point—has been identified, but there could be other possibilities as well. The same conversation for another person may lead to different options, and of course, the manager may have another perspective.

Soft skills work like that – same words can mean different things to different people. It is not easy to achieve specificity, and without that, action is impossible. Generalities do not lead to action.

What can make this process easier?

Consider assessing soft skills by looking for indicators rather than measuring them directly. Most soft skill have various underlying enablers that contribute to their development. For example, the ability to be present requires confidence, courage, clarity, communication, knowledge, warmth, and other factors. Similarly, demonstrating a strategic mindset involves awareness, connecting the dots, articulation, influencing, and more. Communication, which is a foundational enabler for many skills, depends on vocabulary, clarity of thought, the ability to engage, and more. It's essential to consider these underlying enablers because the quality of the ingredients significantly impacts the quality of the product. Some of these enablers may also be more measurable.

Enhancing soft skills is a journey. Begin with small initial actions and gradually add complexity as more nuances emerge. Whatever you perceive as a concern is a suitable starting point. It is a bit like pottery—the potter starts with a concept and some clay, shapes the basic form, examines it from different angles, adds details, and refines the piece repeatedly. The potter also applies glaze and fires it at high temperatures, yet even the final piece can still be improved.

In summary, to develop a soft skill:

1. Introspect: Identify the smallest possible action for change.
2. Practise. Review. Repeat.
3. Once you feel confident, identify the next possible action and continue the cycle of practice, review, and repetition.

Being Firm and Gentle

Leadership is not always about dominance; it's about balance—between firmness and gentleness, clarity and compassion. This article reflects on how leaders can hold their ground without losing their human touch.

A common topic in coaching conversations is about being assertive. Many express feelings like, "I cannot say no", "I dislike having difficult conversations", or "I don't want to spoil relationships." As a result, they often feel overworked, neglected, stressed, or frustrated.

However, assertiveness is more than just the ability to say 'no'; it is essential in various other situations also. It may arise when advocating an idea, requesting resources, or addressing something incorrect that requires change.

Assertiveness starts in the mind. It comes from a well-developed value system and a willingness to stand up for it. It also needs self-confidence, as well as the readiness to handle any consequences that may arise from being assertive. Furthermore, effective communication skills—knowing how to express yourself firmly yet gently—are critical. The way assertiveness is communicated involves both words and tone.

This piece draws on the experience of a senior leader whose intent to be assertive in certain situations was not well supported by her communication skills. Although she was articulate in general, words often eluded her in these contexts. As a result, her choice of words and tone sometimes came across as aggressive. When she asked questions, they seemed accusatory; when she shared her viewpoint, it felt judgemental; and when she advocated for an idea, it appeared too forceful.

To address this, she set out to discover words and phrases that conveyed assertiveness in a firm yet gentle manner. Here are some examples she found useful and added to her conversations, along with a calm, respectful, and understanding tone:

For expressing her needs and boundaries:

- "I understand your perspective, but it's important to me that..."
- "I'm comfortable with... but .... would be a stretch."
- "I'd appreciate it if we could..."
- "We can discuss this, but I do need to prioritise..."
- "I understand your perspective, but we need to proceed with what has been decided."
- "I respect your concern, but we must stay on track with the timeline."
- "I need you to respect my space right now as I focus on my job."
- "It's important that we communicate respectfully, so I'd appreciate it if we could keep the tone calm."
- "I cannot accept this behaviour, but I'm happy to talk about it when we're both calm."

For responding to criticism or disagreement:

- "I appreciate your feedback. I'll give it some thought, but I do hope it is fine if I disagree."
- "I see your point, but I have a different perspective. Let's try to find a solution that works for both of us."
- "I understand you feel that way, but I'm going to have to insist on this decision."
- "I know you want to help, but I've already made up my mind on this."

To set the right expectations:

- "I'm hoping we can agree on..."
- "It's important to me that we both feel comfortable with..."
- "I'd like to establish some ground rules for..."

These tools can be beneficial for everyone, especially when we sometimes feel unable to express our viewpoints. While these phrases can help, it's essential to modify them according to your comfort and what resonates with you. Regular practice is key to mastering this skill.

We also need to work on our tone and body language. What you say is important, but how you say it carries even more weight. The right tone often stems from the right thought process. Being willing to listen, respecting differing opinions, and approaching conversations collaboratively rather than combatively all contribute to achieving the right tone. Additionally, maintaining relaxed, non-threatening body language—complete with a smile and an understanding nod—can significantly enhance your assertiveness.

Blues at Fifty

Turning fifty brings reflection, restlessness, and often a quiet sense of loss. This piece captures the inner turmoil many experience at this mid-life milestone and explores how perspective and purpose can help steady the emotional waters.

Recently, I received a surprise message from someone I had worked with a few years ago. He wanted to have a quick chat, and since I enjoy staying connected with former colleagues, I agreed to speak with him and learn about any impact our work may have had.

When we spoke, his greeting was somewhat perfunctory. Very quickly, he came to the point.

His situation was difficult. He had been let go from his job of over 20 years due to a slowdown. Approaching fifty, he noted, is an age where corporations begin to view you—politely put—differently. He had held a senior position in a large multinational company with a substantial compensation package, but now, after six months of job searching, he was feeling very worried about his prospects. He was considering opportunities within his industry, as he termed it, as well as unrelated fields where he had no experience, and even the possibility of starting his own business.

He had two questions for me:

1. How much time should one allow for finding job openings?
2. Was he missing something in his process of seeking a new career opportunity?

I didn't have definitive answers to these generally broad questions; generic questions can only elicit generic responses. However, we talked for a while, which allowed him to begin finding his own answers.

Here are some points that emerged during our conversation. Some aspects of his approach were effective, while others were not. He also ranked himself on these points on a scale of ten.

Net Fishing

You can fish with a net or with a rod. In his situation, it is prudent for him to cast the net far and wide because his options are limited in "his industry". However, he is fishing with a rod, dangling his resume in a small pond and hoping that someone will bite. Unfortunately, there simply aren't enough fish in his pond. Nevertheless, he is hesitant to cast a wider net due to his concerns. Questions flood his mind: Will it spoil my market worth? Will it look bad on my resume? Am I good enough for other options? These uncertainties are holding him back. (6/10)

Skills First

Experience is what you have done in the past, while your skills determine what you can do in the future. He often discusses his past experiences and projects them well, but he fails to effectively showcase his skills. For example, his ability to develop latent markets, build long-term business relationships, motivate teams, and demonstrate commitment and integrity are not highlighted effectively in his self-description. He speaks at length with pride about his accomplishments, which is fine, but he doesn't spend enough time discussing his skills, strengths, ambition, vision, and what he can achieve. He needs to elaborate on what he can offer prospective employers. (5/10)

Reality Check

He has done well and reached a senior level in his current organisation, with periodic salary and bonus increases. However, there is limited space at the tip of the pyramid. Over time, his cost to the company has outgrown his position, contributing to his decision to move on. To secure a similar level of compensation elsewhere, he must seek a higher position with greater responsibilities. While he is aware of this reality, he continues to pitch himself for lower-level roles, similar to what he was doing earlier, and doesn't express an openness to accept lower packages. Perhaps an element of ego is at play—understandable but not beneficial. (6/10)

Confident Explorer

As he explores unfamiliar territory, discomfort and confidence issues are inevitable. He acknowledges this and tries to exude confidence in discussions. However, he has not engaged in sufficient self-reflection or a SWOT analysis of himself. He hasn't worked enough on building his confidence for new challenges, and he seems unsure that he is ready for such an opportunity. This uncertainty is evident in his mannerisms. He must believe in his ability to succeed in a new arena and, more importantly, be able to convince others of his capability. Knowledge is what you say; how you communicate that knowledge reflects your confidence. He is too focused on the former. (4/10)

On My Own

He expresses a desire to do something on his own, which is both admirable and exciting. Many professionals I have worked with share this aspiration. However, there is one catch: he views this option as a backup plan—something to pursue if he fails to secure a job. This mindset is counterproductive. If he wants to be his own master, he needs to master himself and approach this goal as an equal option. He should make concrete plans, conduct research, assess his resources, and compare this path against traditional employment options. He is yet to take these steps. (4/10)

Patient Negotiator

He is considering job roles that significantly differ from his experience. Such a shift may result in job offers that fall short of his expectations. In many ways, he will need to prove himself again, which requires a patient negotiation process regarding job roles and compensation. However, patience can be challenging in the current climate, making resilience even more critical. While he has not yet received formal offers, he needs to start thinking about navigating this process now. (5/10)

The Blues

Around the age of fifty, many people experience the blues. This is often a time for reflection—a moment to look back on the past and consider the future. With more than half of one's working life behind them, some expectations may have been met while others have not. There are countless ideas swirling around, but energy levels may be waning. The world continues to rush by—it is like watching the scenery change outside a train window while remaining stationary inside. It's challenging to make sense of it all.

Consequently, this is a period for contemplation and determination. The questions "What now?" or "What next?" frequently arise. These inquiries can evoke strong emotions: excitement about new beginnings, frustration about past choices, satisfaction from accomplishing goals, or a mix of many other feelings.

He who was grappling with these thoughts. I allowed him to express his tangled feelings and shared some of my own reflections. It was a helpful exercise. Sometimes, that's all we can do.

I also found myself contemplating how many careers will be affected by the latest wave of technology, particularly artificial intelligence (AI). It's safe to say many will change.

tsunAmI

The flood of information and opinions in today's world can feel overwhelming—like a tsunami. This article explores how digital overload can erode clarity, self-worth, and presence, as well as what it takes to reclaim calm amid the chaos.

In my last post about experiencing the blues at fifty, a reader pointed out that its insights could apply to younger people as well. This prompted me to reflect and conclude that this phenomenon may now also give rise to "blues at twenty-five".

Forty years ago, I made a significant career switch, leaving a respected, stable corporate position for a startup in computer publishing. This was back in 1985 when startups weren't as trendy, and computers were a new concept. Only around 5,000 were sold in India that year, making my decision to edit and publish a computer magazine seem foolish to many—and at times, even to myself.

One of the first editorial pieces I wrote (in June 1985) focused on learning to navigate the evolving world of computers. Even though I was not an expert, I was eager to learn and then share that knowledge with others. Now, four decades later, just replace "computers" with "AI", and the core message remains unchanged. Over the years, we've witnessed numerous waves of technology, but this one feels like a tsunami. Technology is now intricately woven into the fabric of our work and lives—it will impact nearly everyone. While it may feel magical, it is very real.

Here is a picture of that editorial.

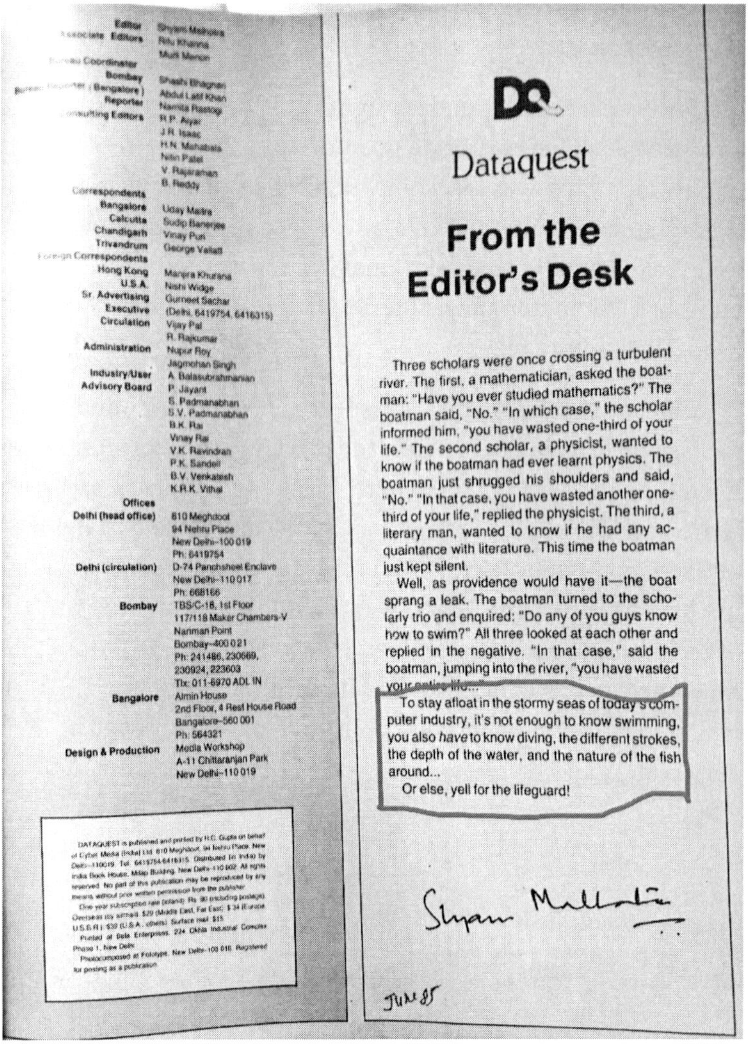

Editor Shyam Malhotra
Associate Editors Ritu Khanna, Murli Menon
Bureau Coordinator
Bombay Shashi Bhagnari
Bureau Reporter (Bangalore) Abdul Latif Khan
Reporter Namita Rastogi
Consulting Editors R.P. Aiyar, J.R. Isaac, H.N. Mahabala, Nitin Patel, V. Rajaraman, B. Reddy
Correspondents
Bangalore Uday Maitra
Calcutta Sudip Banerjee
Chandigarh Vinay Puri
Trivandrum George Vallatt
Foreign Correspondents
Hong Kong Manjira Khurana
U.S.A. Nishi Widge
Sr. Advertising Executive Gurmeet Sachar (Delhi, 6419754, 6416315)
Circulation Vijay Pal, R. Rajkumar
Administration Nupur Roy, Jagmohan Singh
Industry/User Advisory Board A. Balasubrahmanian, P. Jayant, S. Padmanabhan, S.V. Padmanabhan, B.K. Rai, Vinay Rai, V.K. Ravindran, P.K. Sandell, B.V. Venkatesh, K.R.K. Vithal
Offices
Delhi (head office) 810 Meghdoot, 94 Nehru Place, New Delhi–100 019, Ph: 6419754
Delhi (circulation) D-74 Panchsheel Enclave, New Delhi–110 017, Ph: 668166
Bombay TBS/C-18, 1st Floor, 117/118 Maker Chambers-V, Nariman Point, Bombay–400 021, Ph: 241486, 230669, 230924, 223603, Tlx: 011-6970 ADL IN
Bangalore Almin House, 2nd Floor, 4 Rest House Road, Bangalore–560 001, Ph: 564321
Design & Production Media Workshop, A-11 Chittaranjan Park, New Delhi–110 019

DQ

Dataquest

From the Editor's Desk

Three scholars were once crossing a turbulent river. The first, a mathematician, asked the boatman: "Have you ever studied mathematics?" The boatman said, "No." "In which case," the scholar informed him, "you have wasted one-third of your life." The second scholar, a physicist, wanted to know if the boatman had ever learnt physics. The boatman just shrugged his shoulders and said, "No." "In that case, you have wasted another one-third of your life," replied the physicist. The third, a literary man, wanted to know if he had any acquaintance with literature. This time the boatman just kept silent.

Well, as providence would have it—the boat sprang a leak. The boatman turned to the scholarly trio and enquired: "Do any of you guys know how to swim?" All three looked at each other and replied in the negative. "In that case," said the boatman, jumping into the river, "you have wasted your entire life..."

To stay afloat in the stormy seas of today's computer industry, it's not enough to know swimming, you also *have* to know diving, the different strokes, the depth of the water, and the nature of the fish around...

Or else, yell for the lifeguard!

Shyam Malhotra

JUN 85

The usual discussions and arguments about technology and its effects on humankind occur, often accompanied by protests and calls for protection against this substantial disruption. Similar reactions have accompanied previous tectonic technological shifts. While I cannot predict all the pros and cons, I am certain of one thing: change is inevitable, irreversible, and challenging.

Some jobs will be lost, some will be redefined, and new ones will emerge. In which category will you find yourself? You can react when the change hits you, or you can be proactive and ask: What can I do NOW to ride this tsunami and improve my career?

To future-proof your career and adapt to these changes, consider the following actionable strategies:

1. Check Your Status

Investigate how your job will be affected by AI: You might start by consulting AI resources to learn which careers and industries are likely to experience changes. Stay vigilant regarding your organisation's plans, as developments can occur weekly. For instance, I'm currently assessing how the coaching industry will be impacted by AI, and insights from platforms like DeepSeek and ChatGPT have been informative.

Generally, job roles that are repetitive and less complex will be among the first to be affected. Focus on developing skills that AI cannot easily replicate, such as creativity, emotional intelligence, critical thinking, and complex problem-solving, as these will likely be less impacted

2. Embrace Lifelong Learning

Upskill continuously: Invest in yourself. Learning new skills is essential in today's world. It is now non-negotiable to stay updated on the latest trends in AI, automation, and your industry. Platforms like Coursera, Udemy, and others offer a variety of courses on AI, data science, and related fields, catering to different needs and budgets. Even if you're not in a tech role, understanding the fundamentals of AI (e.g., machine learning, natural language processing) will help you work alongside AI tools. If diving into these topics feels overwhelming, at least learn enough to understand how you can use AI in your job or how your organisation intends to use it.

3. Adapt to AI Tools

Leverage AI in Your Work: Most of us won't be involved in developing AI, but we will use it. Learn to use AI-powered tools (e.g., ChatGPT, Microsoft Copilot, Canva AI, Deepseekand many others) to enhance your productivity and efficiency. Remember, those who adopt new tools first are often at an advantage. Familiarise yourself with emerging technologies and their applications in your field. Keep an eye on how AI is impacting your industry and identify areas where you can add value. Join professional communities, attend conferences, and connect with thought leaders in AI innovation. If possible, volunteer for projects involving AI or automation to gain hands-on experience.

I have decided to use AI for some work (including this piece). Recently, I attended a half-day free webinar about AI in Executive Coaching, which left me feeling overwhelmed with information. I created a separate to-do list of 41 points from that one afternoon! While not all of them will be useful, even two or three insights can lead to significant changes for me.

4. Cultivate a Growth Mindset

Be Open to Change: Don't just be open to change; make real changes quickly. Accept that disruption is inevitable and focus on adapting rather than resisting. Explore new ways to integrate

AI into your work or personal projects as soon as you finish reading this!

5. Diversify Your Skill Set

Cross-Disciplinary Knowledge: Combine skills from different fields (e.g., tech + healthcare, design + AI) to create unique value. Many jobs will evolve rather than disappear, so focus on skills that can transition into new roles.

Entrepreneurial Thinking: Consider how you can create new opportunities or businesses in an AI-driven world. Be ready to pivot into new roles or industries as opportunities arise.

6. Build Your Brand

Showcase Your Knowledge: If you're learning about AI and its impact, share your insights. People need to know that you know.

7. Build a Resilient Career

Diversify Income Streams: Explore side hustles, freelancing, or passive income opportunities to reduce your reliance on a single job.

Invest in Personal Branding: Build a strong online presence (e.g., LinkedIn, portfolio) to showcase your skills and adaptability.

8. Focus on Well-Being

Manage Stress: The pace of change can be overwhelming. Prioritise your mental and physical health to stay resilient.

Stay Positive: View AI as an opportunity rather than a threat. It can augment human capabilities and create new possibilities.

Consider exploring some freelancing or passive income options—just in case you need a safety net.

Final Thought

AI is a tool, not a replacement for human potential. By staying adaptable and focusing on what makes us uniquely human, you can not only survive but thrive in the age of AI. The key is to be agile, embrace change, take some risks, and leverage AI to your advantage.

The Stress Virus

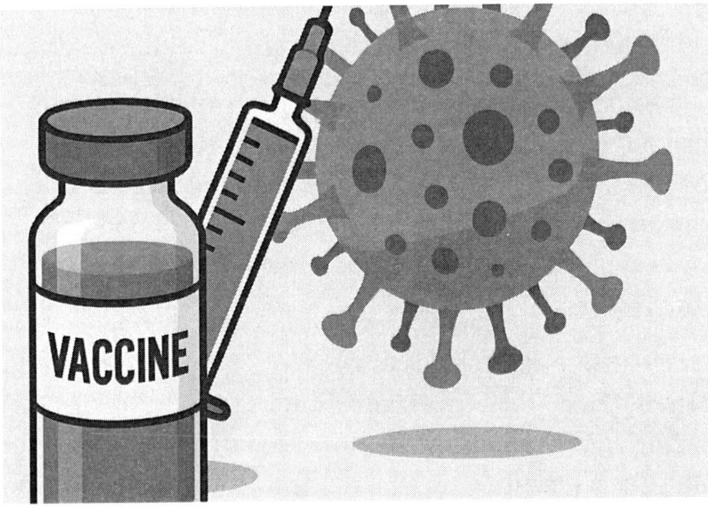

Stress is not a one-size-fits-all experience—it mutates, surprises, and lingers. Through a coaching dialogue, this piece explores how mindset, the ability to pause, and detachment from perfection can build resilience against this modern virus.

Some time ago, after a coaching conversation, I searched online for stress management techniques. Since then, I've received numerous emails about stress from various sources. All of them share one common theme: stress is widespread and its impact is often underestimated. Each source offers a different solution.

The stress virus comes in many variations. It arrives unannounced, behaves differently each time, and when it dissipates, you can never be sure what caused it to do so. There is no known vaccine for stress, so everyone must find their own way to cope. However, some people seem to be more resistant to it than others.

What accounts for this difference? There are two standout reasons: First, their worldview differs from that of others, making them relatively immune to stress. Second, their immediate reactions to stress-inducing situations are more effective. Within these two factors, individuals discover unique answers, which is both the beauty and the tragedy of the situation.

Here is a summary of a stress-related coaching conversation I had recently with Mr X, a senior-level executive in a consulting firm. Like many others, he is: Successful, Ambitious, Aware, Anxious, and Stressed—an embodiment of the acronym SAAAS.

Shyam: HI, how are you today?

Mr X: I'm good, Shyam. A bit stressed, but good.

Shyam: Oh, we will discuss that. But before we do, let's talk about impactful speaking, which we discussed as your development area last time. What has stayed with you since then?

Mr X: The idea of structuring my thoughts into five lines has been helpful, but I struggle to count them subconsciously while speaking. I also feel my messaging could be more polished. Even when meetings go well, I replay them in my mind and think, "I could've said that better."

Shyam: Interesting. You've mentioned your junior team members sometimes over-explain things, and you guide them. Yet, when you're the speaker, you fall into the same trap. Why do you think that happens?

Mr X: Hmm. When I'm the listener, I see the big picture. But as the speaker, I get caught up in details, especially in high-stake moments. I want to convince others, so I tend to say too much, especially in spontaneous situations.

Shyam: So, it's in impromptu situations—like brainstorming calls or unplanned Q&A sessions—where you feel less concise?

Mr X: Exactly. Prepared discussions are fine, but in spontaneous ones, I lose brevity. The pressure to sound intelligent when speaking with seniors makes me verbose, which also causes stress later.

Shyam: As we discussed last time, crispness comes from allowing your thoughts to breathe. How could you create "pause points" in impromptu exchanges?

Mr X: Maybe by asking clarifying questions, like "What part of this should I focus on?" That would give me time to structure my response.

Shyam: That is an option. But if a senior expects an instant reply, how might you frame your response?

Mr X: I could say, "That's an important question—let me think aloud as I piece this together." It sets expectations that I'm processing the output, not just rambling.

Shyam: You referred to this as an "output". What inputs would enhance that output for you?

Mr X: I'm not sure. But I often think that clarity, confidence, and pacing matter. I tend to speak too fast when I'm nervous. Also, word choice—sometimes I use too much jargon.

Shyam: So, slowing down and simplifying are levers you can practise. You also mentioned stress. What about that? You described a meeting where a senior partner criticised you for not keeping him informed. How did that feel?

Mr X: I couldn't explain that the situation was under control and that I didn't want to bother him without a valid reason. My heart was racing. I tried to appear calm on the outside, but inside, I felt rattled. Later, I replayed it endlessly, frustrated I hadn't handled it more smoothly.

Shyam: What worried you most about his reaction?

Mr X: That he'd see me as incompetent or disrespectful. In consulting, perceptions stick. One bad meeting can cast a long shadow over your reputation.

Shyam: And if that shadow lingers? For example, if you have five more tense interactions with him—what's the worst-case outcome?

Mr X: I'd stall in my career. I might even have to leave the firm.

Shyam: And if that happened?

Mr X: (Pauses) I'd find another job. I believe I would get one. I've never struggled career-wise, but the idea of failing here terrifies me.

Shyam: So, the root cause of your stress isn't communication; it's your attachment to this role. What if you could detach slightly?

Mr X: That's easier said than done. However, I see your point: if I'm less fixated on perfection in this role, I'd likely perform better.

Shyam: Yes. Perfection is always a moving goalpost. What mindset change could help you practise being less fixated?

Mr X: By accepting that even if a meeting doesn't go well, it's not catastrophic. I'd still have options, and my self-worth isn't tied to one person's opinion.

Shyam: Exactly. But as we have discussed in the past, the game is finally played on the ground—in the moment. Now, during a stressful situation, how could you shift from a reactive response to a measured one?

Mr X: If I could just pause, that would help. Breathe. Remind myself, "This isn't life or death." I could even visualise the "so what?" chain: "He's upset. So what? I'll clarify later. So what? We'll move on."

Shyam: Beautiful. And in the long-term, what might this bring for you?

Mr X: It could decrease my stress and build emotional resilience. I might also note my triggers and reflect post-meeting—not to criticise myself, but to learn.

Sham: Now, as usual, let's talk about practical steps. The next time stress takes over, what's one action you can take to break the cycle?

Mr X: I could physically step away—get some water, jot down my thoughts, or even message a colleague to vent. I need to interrupt the panic loop. I need to constantly remind myself that perfection is a process, not an event. I cannot stress over each sentence or every moment of criticism. I think I need to detach my sense of self-worth from individual outcomes.

Shyam: Great. Shall we revisit this next month?

Mr X: That works for me. Thanks, Shyam—this has reframed a lot of stuff for me.

Mr X found some answers and possibilities.

What's your virus? And your vaccine?

Managing Your Ego Diet

We all feed our ego—some lavishly, some minimally. This article introduces the concept of an "ego diet" and offers a self-assessment to help you reflect on how your need for recognition and validation impacts your choices and relationships.

Feeding one's ego is as important as feeding one's body. Just like maintaining a balanced diet is crucial for physical health, a balanced ego diet is essential for emotional well-being. An ego that demands excessive feeding can make you feel inflated, prone to collapse with the slightest criticism. On the other hand, an ego with a sparse diet can reduce you to a humble doormat that goes unnoticed.

The ego diet consists of elements such as praise, acknowledgement, recognition, power, influence, titles, private offices, and more.

What do you crave? To help you understand your ego diet, here are 20 introspective questions. Please answer with a simple "yes" or "no"; avoid responses like "sometimes", "I don't think so", or "I don't know".

1. Do you like being the centre of attention?
2. Do you feel envious of people who are receiving attention?
3. Do you seek praise for your accomplishments?
4. Do you feel good about your achievements only when others acknowledge them?
5. When criticised, do you become defensive or dismissive?
6. Do you hold grudges against those who challenge or disagree with you?
7. Do you often compare yourself to others and feel superior?
8. Do you believe you are more capable than most people around you?
9. Do you struggle to admit you could be wrong about something?
10. Do you feel the need to dominate conversations or decisions to maintain your sense of importance?

11. Do you struggle to collaborate unless you are in a leadership role?
12. Do you often steer conversations back to yourself instead of listening deeply to others?
13. Do you feel people "owe" your admiration or loyalty because of who you are?
14. Do you struggle to celebrate others' successes without feeling competitive or envious?
15. Does your mood heavily depend on how others perceive you on a given day?
16. Do you constantly check social media for likes, comments, or validation?
17. If no one notices your efforts, do you feel worthless or resentful?
18. What would you prefer: a high-ranking position or fulfilling job content?
19. Do you frequently mention your power or influence in conversations?
20. Are exclusive perks near the top of your list of desires?

Scoring Your Responses

- Mostly Yes: Your ego may rely heavily on external validation and need constant feeding, indicating you are on a rich and unhealthy ego diet.
- Mixed Responses: You may have a healthy ego but with some areas to improve, or you might have achieved the right balance.
- Mostly No: Your sense of self-worth seems less dependent on external approval, which could indicate you are confident, fulfilled, and content with yourself—or you might be overplaying the humble card.

Difficult Conversations Made Easy

Avoidance makes things worse. Having difficult conversations is essential for growth—both yours and that of others. This article explores how to initiate such discussions with clarity, empathy, and courage, while recognising the emotional landscape both sides must navigate.

A common theme in coaching is the challenge of having tough conversations. When you avoid these discussions, it can be a silent killer. Engaging in a difficult conversation can leave you feeling upset and stressed, while avoidance can lead to frustration and additional stress.

Here are some signs that you may be avoiding a difficult conversation:

- You enter a meeting with a plan to address various issues that have been troubling you, but you leave with almost all of them unsaid.
- You find yourself saying, "Today, I will settle this—enough is enough.".
- After a conversation, you have an internal dialogue, wishing you had made your point more forcefully or spoken up. You might wonder, "Why am I treated like this?" and other similar thoughts.
- You think, "What's the point? He/she will never understand. I might as well give up." Yet, the thought continues to trouble you. These signs may come up repeatedly with certain individuals or in specific situations. Not having difficult conversations can be more frustrating, detrimental, and stressful than having them.

So, how do you classify a conversation as difficult? Difficult conversations typically make both you and others uncomfortable. That discomfort may arise before, during, or even after the conversation. You might worry about unpleasant arguments, raised voices, hurt feelings, potential relationship deterioration, or regretting the discussion later—leading you to avoid the possible confrontation.

Unfortunately, avoiding a conversation does not resolve the issue.

What makes conversations difficult? Several typical causes contribute to the challenge:

- You are discussing grey areas without enough facts or data to prove something conclusively.
- You need to convey bad news that may hurt someone's feelings.
- Your perspective differs significantly from that of the other person.
- The conversation involves negotiation, but neither party is willing to compromise.
- The individuals involved have big egos or sensitive feelings, and you may find yourself in that category, too.
- There is some form of rejection involved in the conversation.
- You are challenging the viewpoints of strong individuals.
- You are dealing with people who resort to emotional blackmail.
- Your needs are not being met, prompting stronger demands.
- You are engaging with argumentative individuals who seek to win every discussion, or you may be that person.

Is there a way to navigate these conversations? To master the art of handling difficult conversations, consider the following steps:

1. Prepare: The first step in having a difficult conversation is getting ready for it. Many people walk in unprepared, hoping for a different outcome. Gather data and organise your thoughts before entering the conversation.

2. Address Smaller Issues First: Tackle smaller disagreements initially. If possible, let go of minor issues.
3. Focus on Emotions: Difficult conversations often involve emotions more than data. Recognise, express, and manage both your emotions and those of the other person involved, without flowing with them.
4. Use Firm but Gentle Language: This is an art form that requires practice.
5. Listen with Empathy: Approach the conversation with concern. Remember, tough conversations don't have to be rude.
6. Watch Your Tone: The content of the conversation is crucial, but how things are said is even more important.
7. Take a Pause: Consider breaking the conversation into multiple segments. Patience and a calm demeanour are essential, as emotions can easily overwhelm the discussion.
8. Acknowledge Multiple Perspectives: Remember that both parties have unique viewpoints, which are valid for them. Remind yourself that proving the other person wrong does not make you right
9. Find Humour: It may be challenging, but humour can ease tension and facilitate smoother conversations.
10. Accept Potential Consequences: Understand that uncomfortable outcomes may arise for both you and the other person, and there may be hurt feelings. This discomfort often underpins the difficulty of the conversation.
11. Take Responsibility: The other person may be difficult, obnoxious, or unreasonable, but you are the one facing the problem. Others may not even realise you're struggling with the conversation. This situation is more

common than you might think. Hoping for a change where the difficult becomes easy is unlikely to happen. Whether you like it or not, it is your responsibility to solve your problem or to live with it.

12. Recognise the Outcome: Recognise the outcome you desire at the end of a difficult conversation. The ideal endpoint is to have a complete dialogue in which no one feels bad, and forward-looking decisions are made. One conversation rarely achieves this. It often requires a series of conversations to reach that point. However, even a small step forward can be useful.

The result of having a difficult conversation can often be satisfying. You may feel a sense of relief and a feeling of accomplishment, even if the problem hasn't yet been resolved. You might also discover that it wasn't as difficult as you initially thought, and that the stories in your mind were just that—stories.

The Clone

Many leaders expect their team members to be their clones. When teams unconsciously replicate their leaders, the diversity of thought suffers. This article highlights the risks of cloning within organisations, and how cultivating openness to dissent and variety can strengthen decision-making and innovation.

Here is a statement I heard a few weeks ago that captures the essence of this issue: "My boss is very accomplished and has great expectations of me. I have been performing well, but I always feel like I'm second best to him. It seems he wants me to be his clone, and this undermines my confidence, especially during meetings with senior stakeholders. What can I do?"

It's completely normal to feel intimidated when comparing yourself to an accomplished boss—especially when it seems like they want you to be a version of themselves.

But here's the key: Your value doesn't lie in being their clone; it's in bringing your unique strengths to the table.

Here are some techniques that can help you reframe this challenge and build confidence in high-stakes situations:

1. Shift Your Mindset from "Second Best" to "Different Strengths":

Your boss has their own style, but so do you. Instead of thinking, "I'll never be as good as them," ask yourself:

- "What do I bring that's different?" (e.g., creativity, analytical depth, relationship-building)
- "How can I complement—rather than replicate—their skills?"

Action: Write down a few strengths you possess that your boss doesn't. Refer to this list before meetings.

2. Redefine "Great Expectations" with Your Boss:

Seek clarity by asking: "I want to meet your expectations—can we align on what success looks like for me in this role?"

Example: If they're a charismatic speaker but you're more data-driven, you could say:

"I may not present the same way you do, but I can ensure our proposals are thoroughly analysed. Does that work for you?"

3. Own Your Seat at the Table (Even When You Feel Like an Imposter):

Before meetings:

- Prepare 1–2 key points to contribute. Even if you're nervous, force yourself to speak early (silence breeds anxiety).
- Use power poses (stand tall, take up space) to trick your brain into feeling confident.

During meetings:

- If you hesitate, pause, take a breath, and speak slower—this projects calm authority.
- If your boss dominates, frame your input as building on theirs:

"To add to [Boss's] point, I'd suggest we also consider [your idea] because..."

4. Build Confidence Through Small Wins:

Start low-risk: Speak up in smaller meetings first, then scale up.

Track successes: Keep a "win log" of times you contributed well—even if it felt small.

Focus on progress, not perfection: Confidence comes from action, not from waiting to feel "ready".

5. Reframe Nervousness as Excitement:

If you feel apprehensive before discussions, remember that the physical symptoms of fear (racing heart, sweating) are the same as those of excitement. So ask yourself: "Am I nervous or excited?" Try telling yourself, "I'm not nervous—I'm energised!" Studies show that this simple reframing can boost performance.

Key Mantra to Internalise:

"Don't try to be the next [Your Boss]. Be the first you."

Final Thought

Your boss's shadow isn't your competition—it's your runway. Use what you learn from them, but trust that your unique mix of skills is why you're there. The more you lean into your authentic strengths, the more confidence (and recognition) you'll gain.

Resolutions!

New Year's resolutions often fizzle out. Why? Because most are wishful intentions, not anchored in reflection or reality. This article shares practical ways to build meaningful resolutions that stick—rooted in purpose, pattern shifts, and emotional energy.

It is that time of the year again—the time for resolutions!

Personally, I can say with complete honesty that the ratio of my successful resolutions to failed ones is rather low. This isn't a great ratio, so I spent some time reflecting on it and gathered a set of reasons why my resolutions seem to fail repeatedly. I suspect that my reasons may be similar to those of many others.

Of course, excuses often masquerade as reasons.

Wish Lists

I have found that my resolutions often resemble wish lists. They consist of things that float around in my mind as desires, but there is often no serious intent to achieve them. To make it worse, many of these lists come from external expectations. For example, my wife might say that this year we should visit new destinations where everyone is going, and suddenly it becomes my resolution. A friend may work hard to prepare for a marathon, and voilà, it becomes my resolution, too.

These wish lists arise from cultural expectations, social pressures, FOMO, or other hard-to-pin-down influences. They can be spontaneous thoughts or long- dormant ideas. Either way, there is little thought put into them before turning them into resolutions.

I've noticed that I often set resolutions that are too daunting. For instance, I might resolve to trek to Everest Base Camp this year before it's too late. While it's a positive goal, I feel the need to clear all my smaller tasks first so I can fully focus on the trip. The problem is that the small tasks keep piling up, and my resolution suffers as a result.

Some goals are far too distant in terms of time. For example, I often resolve to author three books within the next five years.

This has been a recurring aspiration—a rolling five- year plan. Since there's so much time to complete it, I keep putting off the start for "another day".

I have also found that many of my resolutions are too vague. A resolution to "work on fitness" or "reduce stress" leaves me unsure of my progress, as I do not have a measure. I may begin an activity, but then, after a week or two, it fades into the background of everyday life.

Lastly, I tend to set too many resolutions, trying to make up for those I've previously broken. The lost years feel like they need recovery, and I spend the year figuring out which resolution to tackle first.

Stop before Start

Often, I make resolutions to start new habits but neglect to resolve to stop doing things that hinder my progress. For instance, I want to be fit but don't change my eating habits. I aim to be assertive at work but am not prepared to face the consequences. I resolve to let go of certain responsibilities but struggle to trust others with them. Frequently, starting something new requires stopping something else, yet this step is often overlooked.

Get Real

I tend to overestimate the positive outcomes (as I've been encouraged to stay optimistic) while underestimating the costs, risks, and obstacles associated with my new resolutions (while avoiding pessimism). In this dance between optimism and realism, I often lose sight of what's realistic and, consequently, so do my resolutions.

Déjà vu

Has it become customary to make resolutions at the start of the year? Or is it a trend past its prime? Why not consider making meaningful resolutions on other days? Despite feeling a sense of déjà vu, I find myself engaging in this ritual year after year.

Clean Slate

Perhaps it is time to start afresh. Instead of making half-hearted resolutions, maybe I should aim to make resolutions with genuine intent.

The Art of Peer Management

Managing former peers or equals is one of leadership's trickiest transitions. This piece offers insights into navigating new dynamics, building credibility without arrogance, and blending authority with camaraderie.

Contrary to popular belief, your team is not just comprised of the individuals who report directly to you. It also includes the colleagues with whom you regularly collaborate, who may not fall under your direct supervision. Often, these colleagues constitute your A-team, as you cannot accomplish significant tasks without their input and support. Effectively managing peers is frequently an underemphasised skill, especially when considering the number of meetings with peers a manager attends each day. In each meeting or discussion, managing peers plays a crucial role, particularly in flat, matrix organisations. Peer management is a nuanced skill that often requires a delicate balance of assertiveness, diplomacy, and collaboration. While traditional management typically involves hierarchical relationships, peer management necessitates a more horizontal approach. This means influencing and guiding colleagues at a similar level without formal authority.

One of my clients is a young manager in a global organisation. She is a digital marketing specialist who has been hired for her in- depth knowledge and understanding of the market. Her peers in the organisation are the traditional marketers who have been with the company for many years. Many of them are far senior in age and feel they ought to be respected for past achievements. Although they recognise the need to adapt to the new methods being adopted, they simultaneously resist them, often feeling threatened by their rapid implementation. Her challenge is to motivate them to accept and work with new ideas. She senses that she is often judged, not well-liked, and regularly undermined in discussions. Commitments to new plans are often either not made or not kept.

There are several dynamics at play here:

1. Professional Rivalry: While healthy competition can drive performance, unhealthy rivalry may hinder teamwork and overall productivity.
2. Power Struggles: Subtle power dynamics can emerge, particularly when resources or recognition are limited.
3. Personality Clashes: Different work styles and communication preferences can lead to misunderstandings and friction.
4. Historical Baggage: Past experiences, both positive and negative, can impact current interactions.

Given these challenges, the obvious question arises: What does she need to do to fulfil her role effectively?

During our discussions, several behaviour-based strategies emerged. Here are some examples, which are not necessarily in order:

Q: Can you describe a time when you had to resolve a conflict with a peer? How did you handle the situation, and what was the outcome?

A: I explained what had been planned and requested that he complete the task as soon as possible. He responded that he didn't have time to take on this new task and questioned why I always approached him at the last moment. I tried to clarify that I had also received this information on short notice from my manager. Unfortunately, not much was accomplished after that.

Q: Can you share an example of a time when you successfully influenced a peer to adopt a new idea or approach?

A: It turned out to be less difficult than I anticipated once I figured out what he wanted. He was concerned about whether he would receive additional resources and recognition for the work but was too proud to ask for it. By reading between the lines, I understood his needs and approached my manager, who agreed to the same. After that conversation, it was relatively simple to move forward.

Q: How do you approach situations where you disagree with a peer? Can you provide a specific example?

A: I frequently encounter such situations. Once I became aware of the nuances of peer management, I started experimenting with different styles. When a strong disagreement arises and the issue is significant, I try to understand my peer's perspective and employ a give-and-take approach. Finding middle ground is often effective. In cases of mild disagreement, I present more data and facts to support my viewpoint. Sometimes, I simply agree to move past the disagreement, using the opportunity to build rapport and goodwill for future interactions.

Some enablers and derailers of effective peer management can be observed in the statements above. Here are some qualities of great peer managers:

1. Empathy: They understand and consider the feelings and perspectives of their peers, promoting a supportive and inclusive environment. This ability helps them build strong relationships, which can be crucial in managing difficult situations and fostering collaboration.
2. Effective Communication: They are skilled communicators who express their ideas clearly and listen actively. This helps in reducing misunderstandings and building trust. They can negotiate effectively and find diplomatic solutions. When necessary, they can assert themselves and present their case tactfully

while maintaining clarity and conciseness in their communication to leave little room for ambiguity.

3. Collaborative Spirit: Great peer managers promote teamwork and collaboration. They value input from all team members and encourage collective problem-solving. They respect their peers, even if they disagree or possess greater expertise in certain areas. They handle conflicts calmly and constructively, focusing on solutions rather than placing blame. Additionally, they can effectively motivate and inspire others, rallying the team towards common goals.
4. Flexibility and Adaptability: Effective managers can adjust their approach based on the needs of the team and changing circumstances, making them well-suited for dynamic environments.
5. Integrity: They act with honesty and uphold ethical principles, which earns them respect and credibility among their peers. They strive to build trust and rapport, fostering mutual respect.
6. Goal-Oriented: Effective managers keep the team focused on objectives and results, ensuring that everyone is aligned towards achieving common goals.
7. Managing Personality Clashes: These managers excel at seeking common ground and identifying areas of agreement to promote cooperation. They remain open to mediation by third parties when necessary and maintain a professional demeanour in difficult situations to effectively manage personality clashes.
8. Positive Attitude: Great managers typically maintain a positive attitude, which helps them avoid ego-related issues. Their optimistic outlook can be contagious, boosting the morale of the entire team.

9. Politically Savvy: While they avoid office politics, they are keenly aware of the political and cultural dynamics within the organisation. They navigate these complexities sensitively, without becoming overly enmeshed themselves.
10. Change Agents: Effective managers are skilled change agents who involve peers in decision-making processes, helping everyone feel part of the solution. They explain the benefits of their objectives clearly. Above all, they are patient and persistent.

Managing peers can be a complex but rewarding endeavour. With mindfulness and practice, it can become a significant asset for any manager.

Top Ten Self-Saboteurs

We sometimes block our own path through procrastination, perfectionism, or fear of success. This piece highlights self-sabotaging patterns and how awareness, reframing, and self-compassion can help break the cycle.

In coaching, a common question is, "How do you think you sabotage yourself?" This question can be difficult to answer, as many people are unaware of their behaviours, while others may hesitate to disclose them.

Follow-up questions like those below can help clarify their responses:

- What do you feel angry about with yourself?
- What tasks have you postponed for an extended period?
- What obstacles hinder your goal achievement?
- What qualities do you frequently wish you possessed?
- What negative words do you use to describe yourself?

At its core, self-sabotage refers to behaviours or thought patterns that hold an individual back from achieving their desires. It can represent a serious condition or a disruptive pattern that an individual has come to believe about themselves.

Curiosity led me to explore patterns in the responses shared during coaching conversations. I categorised these responses into ten groups, noting that there is some overlap:

1.Over Thinking

I think too much, overanalyse situations, and struggle to make decisions. I constantly seek more data.

2. Micro-Management

I find it difficult to prioritise, often get lost in detail, and typically feel rushed for time. I tend to over-plan and can't let go of minor tasks.

3. Impatience

I struggle to wait for tasks to be completed and often rush into them. I check progress frequently and become easily irritated.

4. Ego

I become upset when questioned, resist feedback, and react aggressively to challenges. My self-image is fragile, leading me to lose interest if challenged by a superior. I dwell on past insults for too long.

5. Perfectionism

I strive for perfection, often spending excessive time on tasks, leading to missed schedules. I am rarely satisfied and can be overly critical of those around me. I beat myself up for perceived non-achievements and frequently ask too many questions, struggling with ambiguity.

6. Procrastination

I delay decisions until the last moment and often revisit choices. I lag on schedules and tend to wait to see what others think before acting. Fear of risk causes me to postpone decisions.

7. Lack Of Trust

I struggle to trust my team, often viewing new people as incompetent. I've difficulty collaborating and frequently double-check what my peers say, believing that people can be fundamentally lazy.

8. Giving Up

I tend to give up too soon and struggle to assert myself. This leads to frustration, fatigue, and a reluctance to follow up.

9. Lack of Listening

I find it hard to maintain my attention, leading people to avoid discussing matters with me. I jump to conclusions and have difficulty reading the room or understanding unspoken cues.

10. Looking good

I try too hard to look good. I don't question decisions. I agree with my seniors and avoid taking on difficult tasks. I also tend not to take risks.

Question: What would your response be if asked the same question? Which group(s) do you identify with? Your answer could be something outside this list as well. And remember, don't overthink it!

The Stool of Upsets

Upsets are rarely caused by a single factor. This article introduces a metaphorical "three-legged stool" composed of expectations, intentions and communication which serves the structural roost of our emotional disruptions. Understanding this stool can help reduce reactivity and build perspective.

Werner Erhard of the Landmark Forum identified three main causes of upset:

- Undelivered Communication
- Thwarted Intentions
- Unmet Expectations

I first encountered these concepts in a Landmark Forum programme about 30 years ago. It helped me realise that I must work on my upsets—no one else can or will. They are my upsets, and I own them.

Undelivered Communication

Undelivered communication refers to messages, information, or feedback that are not conveyed, often festering internally or failing to reach their intended audience. They may be ignored or not effectively acted upon. When you withhold truths, the words left unsaid can echo for a long time. These are your upsets, some lingering for years, while others fade quickly. Although this applies to all areas of life, the examples I share often arise in coaching conversations:

- You want to express many things but feel you never get the chance.
- You have opportunities to speak but still don't voice your thoughts, leading to greater frustration with yourself than with anyone else.
- You send numerous emails that go unread or are ignored.
- You propose many ideas that are either dismissed or not acted upon, making you feel unheard.
- You give instructions that are misunderstood or deemed vague, leading to a sense of being constantly misinterpreted.

Undelivered communication creates misalignment and frustration, leading to upsets. There are only two ways to avoid these negative consequences: 1. Speak up. Clearly and impactfully articulate your thoughts or concerns. Don't sit on your ideas or complaints—taking the risk is better than remaining silent indefinitely.

2. Don't shy away from following up, repeating yourself, and being assertive. Demand accountability when necessary.

You can choose between the risk of upsetting others or remaining upset yourself. The choice is yours.

Thwarted Intentions

Thwarted intentions in corporate life occur when well-meaning plans, initiatives, or individual efforts are blocked, undermined, or fail due to organisational barriers, office politics, or misalignment. Such plans, drawn up in hope, can be erased in fear or frustration, leading to disenchantment and upsets. Here are some common examples and possible solutions:

1. Innovation Stifled by Bureaucracy: You propose a streamlined process using automation, but leadership insists on sticking to legacy systems because "that's how things have always been done."
    - Possible solution: Propose your idea as a small-scale "experiment" (e.g., "Let's test this in one department for 30 days"), framing it as a temporary, low-risk trial to bypass resistance to big changes (The Trojan Horse Pilot).
2. Promotions Denied Despite Merit: You are told you are good enough to be promoted, but the company favours tenure over skill or is influenced by office politics.

   - Possible Solution: Before the review discussion, gather data showcasing your achievements and share it with all concerned, emphasising the discrepancy between policy and reality.

3. Budget Cuts Killing Strategic Projects: After months of development, your new product loses funding at the last minute due to short-term cost-saving measures or because the new manager has a different growth strategy.

   - Possible Solution: Keep the project alive by volunteering some time for its development, putting it on the back burner rather than abandoning it entirely, as there's always a chance it can be revived.

4. Change Initiatives That Go Nowhere: You announce improvements for the future, but your team resists change and subverts the initiative.

   - Possible Solution: Introduce the change in small, frequent doses instead of large launches. Use peer ambassadors instead of top-down mandates to enrol people rather than order them.

5. Training Programmes with No Real Impact: You organise training sessions, but the team struggles to apply what they've learned due to day-to-day workload pressures.

   - Possible Solution: Acknowledge that about 70% of training knowledge is lost within 24 hours. To combat this, implement recaps and use training buddies to increase accountability.

6. Burnout from Unrealistic Expectations: Leadership tells you to "work smarter, not harder", yet continues to pile on last-minute requests without adjusting deadlines.

   – Possible Solution: Emphasise the consequences of last-minute requests, including implications like project delays and team burnout. Sometimes, what is obvious to you is not apparent to others, so practise firm but gentle rebuttals.

7. Collaboration Efforts Blocked by Silos: While collaboration is essential, conflicting performance indicators often lead your peers and you to prioritise personal goals over the company's overall success.

   – Possible Solution: Consider exchanging resources and supporting the KPIs of your peers. There is a cost to maintaining collaboration on your end, but there are benefits as well. Avoid falling into the ego trap of thinking, "They aren't helping, so why should I?"

8. Strategy is the First Casualty: Although you work toward a stated long-term vision, you often face pressure to deliver short-term results.

   – Possible Solution: Short- term goals focus on spending, while long-term goals emphasise investment. Both aspects must be balanced. Highlight the long-term costs associated with short-term decisions, using data and factual evidence wherever possible.

The underlying principles for countering thwarted intentions include:

- Make Inaction More Painful Than Action: For example, expose the hidden costs of maintaining the status quo.
- Bypass, Don't Attack: Work around obstacles instead of confronting them head-on.
- WeaponizeData: Use hard numbers rather than opinions to support your points.

Be Assertive and Increase Your Influence: The risks associated with not being assertive can be much higher.

Unmet Expectations

Unmet expectations in corporate life are the third leg of the stool of upsets. These expectations can create silent pressures to be more, perform more, achieve more, and deliver more. Sometimes these pressures are realistic; at other times, they are not.

Here are some common expectations that arise in my practice:

1. You may expect your manager to coach and mentor you in every situation, while your manager believes in letting employees learn independently.
2. You might want your manager to grant you autonomy, but your manager prefers to keep a close watch on details and likes to stay "on top of things".
3. In your view, young people should be hardworking and ambitious, while many team members prefer to take it easy and contribute minimally.
4. You expect your work to speak for itself and for you to receive recognition, but the organisation may overlook your contributions.

5. You seek clear directions on desired outcomes, but the organisation's uncertain environment results in constantly shifting goals.
6. You hope your team will be self-motivated and proactive, but they may not yet be ready for that level of responsibility.
7. You believe your manager should communicate frontline issues to top leadership, but your manager tends to play it safe and remain conservative.
8. You are accustomed to a process-driven work structure in your previous job and expect the same in your new role, but the startup culture differs significantly.
9. You expect your team to take independent responsibility and inform you if problems arise, but they prefer to keep their issues to themselves.
10. You value proactivity in problem-solving rather than waiting for directives, yet your second-in-command views this approach as risky.

There may be additional expectations as well.

Keep in mind that these are your expectations. Others are not obligated to meet them. If anything, it is your responsibility to motivate others to support your expectations.

Not all expectations are realistic, and it's crucial to distinguish between well-thought-out goals and wish lists.

Expectations should be recalibrated periodically, aligning them upwards or downwards based on the current reality, which can change rapidly.

This three-legged stool is a weight you bear; it makes no promises of comfort. Are you sitting on one?

Tanya's Challenge: Building Senior Presence

What sets senior leaders apart? It's not just expertise—it's their presence. This article outlines subtle, learnable shifts in body language, tone, and narrative that can create credibility, command attention, and build gravitas.

A young lady I work with (let's call her Tanya) is striving to develop a "senior presence". She works at a large global consulting firm and is bright, articulate, and capable. However, she feels a lack of experience when interacting with senior client stakeholders who have "three times the experience she has". Additionally, she faces seniors from her own organisation in these meetings. This dynamic leads her to feel inadequate and "judged" for her responses, negatively impacting her growth in "a highly competitive environment". As a result, she often remains quiet, which, in turn, affects her career advancement. It's a challenging situation.

Here is a summary of a conversation with her:

Shyam: In the pre- coaching questionnaire, you mentioned feeling insecure during interactions with senior stakeholders, and how that holds you back from speaking up. You've also expressed concerns about being judged and how that might impact your career. What would you like to focus on today to move forward?

Tanya: I feel like I don't have the same presence as more experienced leaders, and sometimes I doubt whether my contributions are valuable. I fear saying the wrong thing, so I tend to stay quiet, but then I worry that makes me invisible. This is causing a lot of stress for me. I have received feedback that I should work with a coach to build a senior presence.

Shyam: It sounds like you're struggling between wanting to contribute meaningfully and fearing negative judgement. If we could do just one thing to help you feel better in these interactions, what would that be?

Tanya: I don't know. I either don't speak at all, or I speak very quickly and blurt out what I want to say. Then I feel ignored if no one acknowledges me. I also worry that people might ask follow- up questions and I won't have the answers. If I could just make valid points, I'd be more likely to speak up and appear more senior.

Shyam: Has anyone suggested that your ideas aren't valid?

Tanya: No, I don't think so. I believe I make some good points. I compare myself to those senior leaders with so much expertise and think, "Why would they listen to me?"

Shyam: Interesting. What if, instead of comparing your experience to theirs, you considered your unique perspective as someone younger and knowledgeable in your field?

Tanya: Hmm… I do notice things they miss, like how younger teams respond to policies or tech trends with which they might be less familiar. In fact, two senior client stakeholders are struggling with current trends as per their own team members. But that doesn't seem good enough; they have so much more experience.

Shyam: That sounds promising. So, if you were to position yourself as someone who bridges their gap with current trends, how might that change your presence?

Tanya: Maybe I could prepare a few key points where my perspective adds value, instead of waiting to be asked. But I find that very challenging, especially when my seniors are present.

Shyam: That sounds like a proactive step. Remember, you have also been invited to the meeting – you have not gate-crashed. So, ideas are expected from you. Is there a particular idea that you can test in your next meeting?

Tanya: I could identify one topic where I know I have an interesting viewpoint and speak up early, before I overthink it.

Shyam: Yes. Overthinking is an impediment at times. By the time we have processed our thoughts, the moment may have passed. Would you need any support to make this happen?

Tanya: Maybe if I rehearsed with a colleague first, I'd feel more confident.

Sham: Great idea. If it is fine by you, I would like to explore one more thing with you: this feeling of being judged. What's the worst that could happen if someone disagrees with you?

Tanya: I guess they might think I'm not capable… and that could impact my growth.

Shyam: And how do you think your growth will be affected if you do not speak up and add value often enough?

Tanya: That could also be seen as negative. By speaking up, they might believe in me and respect me more."

Shyam: Exactly. And if they respect you more, how does that change your presence?

Tanya: Then I'd be seen as a leader, not just a junior person. That's what I want!

Shyam: So, to summarise: You would like to prepare one key insight for your next meeting, rehearse it, and speak up early. You will also try and recognise that your perspective holds unique value which can help you. How does that feel?

Tanya: It feels doable—and exciting.

Shyam: What one word would describe how you want to show up moving forward?

Tanya: "Assertive"? Not silent, not aggressive—just confidently myself.

Shyam: That's great! Let's check in next time on how being "assertive" went for you.

Seniority does not come with age alone; it also comes with presence, which cannot be built by remaining silent.

Old Wisdom: "It is better to keep your mouth shut and appear stupid than open it and remove all doubt."

New Wisdom: "It is better to speak up and share your ideas rather than keep silent and let others assume you have none."

PVR and the Drama Triangle

Not all drama unfolds on screen. The Drama Triangle—Persecutor, Victim, Rescuer—is a common leadership trap. This article explores how recognising your role in this dynamic can help you shift to healthier, more empowered patterns.

In India, 'PVR' is a chain of multiplexes. In the context of cinema, PVR stands for Priya Village Roadshow, formed as a joint venture between Priya Exhibitors Private Limited and Village Roadshow Limited, an Australian entertainment company. However, this piece is not about movies and the triangles in them but about another type of drama in which we all are willing or unwilling participants – every day.

In this drama, PVR stands for Perpetrator, Victim, and Rescuer. The Drama Triangle, identified by a U.S. therapist Stephan Karpman, consists of three primary roles: The Victim, who feels oppressed and helpless; the Persecutor, who blames and criticises others; and the Rescuer, who tries to save the day without being asked. These roles are not fixed; individuals can shift between them in various situations, an aspect that often comes up in coaching conversations.

These three roles stem from underlying beliefs and offer certain benefits to the person playing them, but there is often a significant price to be paid. Typically, the costs outweigh the benefits. However, each role also holds the potential for transformation into true leadership through self-awareness, responsibility, and empowerment. The challenge lies in being mindful of which role you have adopted –whether consciously or unconsciously – and discovering the path to true leadership from there.

Perpetrator (Persecutor)

A perpetrator is someone who dominates, blames, or attacks others, often to maintain control, driven by the belief that they are surrounded by incompetent people. This role thrives on power and aggression, creating fear or oppression. While typically viewed as negative, a perpetrator's traits—such as decisiveness and assertiveness—can be redirected positively.

If you find yourself playing this role, you can evolve by shifting from a control mindset to an influence mindset. This involves figuring out how to enrol people to your perspective and focusing on acts that inspire instead of using fear tactics. True leadership requires humility—recognising that authority should empower, not intimidate. By channelling your assertiveness into mentorship and advocacy, you can become a strong and ethical leader who drives change rather than conflict.

Victim

The victim feels powerless, oppressed, or helpless, often believing that they have no control over their circumstances. They may see everyone as an enemy—out to get them—which leads to increased dependence and stagnation.

If in some situations you find yourself in this role, remind yourself that wherever you are, you can choose to move to another place. Remember that this is just a role; it does not define you. You can transform into a leader by embracing resilience. By taking ownership of your situation and using your experience to empathise with others, you can change yourself as well.

True leaders who once played the victim role often emerge as advocates, transforming their pain into purpose. By developing confidence and problem-solving skills, they inspire others to overcome adversity, becoming symbols of hope and perseverance.

Rescuer

The rescuer steps in to save others, often at the expense of their own needs, sometimes even when no one has asked for help. While their intentions are noble, rescuers can inadvertently enable dependency rather than growth. Their desire to "fix" others may stem from a need for self-validation, which can result in them being seen as meddlers.

If you have donned this mantle, you may be supporting victims or trying to reform perpetrators, believing you are helping. In reality, you could be pushing others deeper into their circumstances, contrary to your intentions. It's essential to shift from being a saviour to being a supporter, which fosters independence rather than dependency.

By setting boundaries for support and encouraging self-sufficiency, former rescuers can become transformational leaders who build capacity in others rather than creating reliance.

Each role—perpetrator, victim, rescuer—has the potential to transform into effective leadership when individuals move from dysfunction to empowerment. A perpetrator becomes a leader through influence, a victim through resilience, and a rescuer through empowerment.

The Big Bad Boss

Most stories about "bad bosses "overlook the systemic context. This article deconstructs the mythology of the toxic boss, prompting reflection on patterns, perceptions, and how leadership behaviours can evolve—and sometimes distort—under pressure.

Managing a difficult boss is a challenge encountered by about 10% of my coachees. When it arises, it is often an intense and significant issue. A poor relationship with the boss can be demotivating and create major obstacles in one's career. If not addressed, these relationships can also have serious emotional consequences.

Here are some descriptions of problematic bosses I have heard from people I have coached over the last decade:

- Allows no freedom
- Gives unclear instructions and blames others later
- Never praises – only criticises, which damages my self esteem
- Sets unrealistic targets just to be vindictive
- Does not respect my time and expects work at all hours
- Is biased and supports others, but not me
- Takes credit for all good work and shifts blame to others
- Claims to empower but simply dumps responsibility
- Works all the time and expects the same from me
- Provides inconsistent instructions and is completely incompetent
- Just does not listen to anything
- Is very sarcastic and makes me feel foolish

And don't think that is the end of the list; I am sure there are more.

But this discussion isn't solely about the boss; it's about you and how you react to or manage your boss.

Whether you like it or not, managing your boss is a necessity. It's surprising how many people have never seriously considered how and why they need to manage their boss.

Those who effectively manage their bosses often possess the following ten qualities. There may be others, but these work for most people:

1. They genuinely accept the responsibility of managing their boss, viewing it as part of their job. For them, the boss relationship is just one of many relationships, and both parties must put in effort. It takes mutual understanding to make things work. If you accept this, many of Steps 2 -9 become easier.
2. They recognise that their boss is just another human being with similar aspirations, challenges, and stress points. Understanding this allows them to see the whole person. They can sense moods, trigger points, social style, and cultural preferences and adjust their responses accordingly with empathy and confidence, focusing on significant issues rather than trivial matters.
3. They do not view situations in black and white. They understand the nuances involved in decisions and discussions, which helps them appreciate their boss's perspective and enhances their ability to manage the relationship. They accept that between the right and the wrong there is often a maybe.
4. They have a growth mindset. They focus on feedback from the boss rather than how it's delivered, viewing it as a necessary but sometimes difficult aspect of personal development. This requires emotional maturity.
5. They recognise that no one is purely good or bad, including their boss. They strive to emphasise the positives while managing the negatives—much like cholesterol—practising this approach daily.
6. They engage in open and honest conversations with their boss and are proactive about discussing any issues. They don't wait for the boss to approach them first.

7. They understand that sometimes difficult conversations with the boss are necessary regarding decisions, promotions, schedules, and more. They possess the courage and skills to navigate these discussions.
8. They maintain a friendly professional relationship with their boss but recognise that they should not become friends. This distinction helps keep the relationship pleasant yet professional.
9. They understand that the boss is not always right but avoid openly contradicting them. Instead, they find alternative ways to convey their concerns.
10. They are comfortable asking for help if the relationship becomes too challenging, whether it's from colleagues, HR, or higher-ups. They see this as a sign of strength, not weakness.

Suggestion: Go back and read from the top again but replace "They" with "I". Give yourself an honest ranking, and you might discover some insights about yourself.

Remember, there is no absolute scale for these qualities. No matter where you stand, there's always room for improvement. One can move on too, but keep in mind, another boss will always be there to manage.

Feelings and Emoticons

Feelings shape behaviour, but naming and expressing them is often harder than it seems. This article explores how emotional awareness, articulation, and vocabulary can empower better coaching, decision-making, and connection. It highlights why 'managing' feelings beats suppressing them.

In coaching, identifying and addressing feelings is a significant part of the process, as emotions can either provide energy or drain it. A substantial amount of coaching revolves around feelings, as they drive our actions and behaviours – often without our knowledge. Even what we consider 'logical decisions' are invariably influenced by our emotions, whether we acknowledge it or not.

We live with our feelings constantly, yet capturing and expressing them can be quite challenging. It is like finding the perfect emoticon—most available options do not fully capture our thoughts. First, we often struggle to recognise our feelings, and second, we lack the vocabulary to express them. If you ask someone, "How do you feel today?" the responses you'll typically receive are limited to words like good, happy, bored, sad, angry, tired, or excited. This shows that we find it difficult to capture feelings and articulate them, which may hinder our ability to manage and harness them effectively. Often, the phrase "control your feelings" is used, but control implies suppressing feelings, which is neither possible nor advisable. Feelings should be managed, not controlled. Articulating them is only the first step—which, as discussed earlier, can be challenging. Acknowledging them is the second step, and acting on them purposefully is the third. Feelings exist, they are real, and they belong to us. There is nothing wrong with feeling a certain way; the issue lies instead in the behaviour that follows, which needs to be managed

When we try to identify feelings, we often describe what happened or what is likely to happen, focusing more on the causes than the emotions themselves. I often ask clients (and myself) to express their feelings in two or three words. This can be a difficult question to answer. The classic terms like sad, mad, or glad are often insufficient; clients might respond with uncertainty or feelings of being in between. Simple phrases can also be lacking–saying "I feel stupid" might encompass anger, indifference, or fear. The emotions that require discovery and management in coaching, along with some words that may express them, include:

- Fear – apprehensive / doubtful / uncertain / restless / confused / lost / scared
- Anger – angry / frustrated/ disturbed/ cheated / pained
- Indifference – helpless / demotivated / bored / giving up / pointless / empty / sad
- Empowered – looking forward / energetic / ready to go / excited / curious
- Happiness – celebratory / satisfied / joyful / good

You ideally want to operate with the last two emotions.

The Impact of the Virus

Working from home isn't just about location; it's a mindset shift. This piece, drawn from coaching conversations during the pandemic, offers 10 grounded tips to maintain rhythm, resilience, and relationships when the lines between work and life blur. While the pandemic has ended, some effects remain, perhaps etched in our lives forever.

The flavour of coaching – like everything else in the world – has shifted due to the impact of the virus. Many of my clients have been working from home for the last few years Some have adapted easily, while others have faced challenges. Our discussions naturally revolved around these developments, as there is a good chance that this situation may continue for some time.

Here are some insights shared by my clients, compiled from our conversations:

1. Establish a Routine: Working from home is not the same as working anytime at home. A routine is useful—some even insist it is essential. Set specific hours and stick to them, including normal official working hours, like nine to five. Bottom line: establish a routine and make every effort to adhere to it.
2. Communicate Your Work Hours: If you live with others, they must know when you're working. Be prepared for occasional, curious interruptions—children visiting during a video call, a dog barking, or your spouse asking you to answer the door. Such disturbances should not be more disruptive than unexpected phone calls or urgent meetings at the office but somehow are so. The mind requires retraining to handle these interruptions swiftly.
3. Create a Dedicated Workspace: Most people recommend having a small desk to work from, as the dining table is not suitable. If space allows, make this choice. One client regrettably gave the study to their children, which led to mixed feelings.
4. Dress for Success: A few clients found that dressing for work helped their mindset. Working in pyjamas or shorts didn't promote productivity, so it's worth

experimenting to find what makes you most comfortable and focused.

5. Adapt Your Environment: Clients mentioned their home environment was not conducive to work. Offices have an air of professionalism that homes lack. Try to create a bit of an office ambience at home, if possible. Your mindset needs to adapt to the new environment to stay productive.
6. Overcome Technical Challenges: Normal IT support is often unavailable while working from home. If your internet is slow, software updates occur unexpectedly, or Microsoft teams play truant, you are on your own. One client had to conduct a presentation using WhatsApp from their balcony for better connectivity. Familiarising yourself with your devices can be beneficial.
7. Embrace Self-Sufficiency: The absence of support systems, like tea services or cafeterias, means you must adapt quickly. Cultivate a "do it yourself" mentality.
8. Respect Household Routines: Remember, a home operates on its own set of rules. Cleaning happens at 11 a.m., the vegetable vendor arrives at 3 p.m., and you might run out of water in the afternoon. Your work routine needs to fit around these household schedules.
9. Manage Loneliness: One client, who lives alone, managed the logistics of cooking and cleaning, but found the loneliness overwhelming. No amount of video calls with friends and family helped. She said she had never missed her domestic staff more. Feeling ungrateful compared to colleagues with no such options (she works in the India office of a European company), she resolved not to complain until May 3, 2020, when the lockdown was projected to end.

10. Create Work-Life Balance: Another senior manager, typically a workaholic, said the lack of social activities led him to work harder. His globally dispersed team, which is also working from home, had no distractions—parties, gym, dates, or eating out—so keeping pace with them became a bit of a nightmare. He committed to a bit of off-time, ensuring it wasn't spent worrying about virus updates or watching news debates.

The overarching message that emerged from our coaching conversations is simple: be adaptable, accept the reality, and move on. However, simple answers are often not easy to implement.

The Rusted Blades

In the churn of corporate restructuring, mid-career professionals often face sudden layoffs. This article highlights the 'rusted blades'—valued yet sidelined individuals—and suggests steps organisations must take to grow, prepare, or transition these employees with fairness, foresight, and dignity.

I have had the unfortunate experience of providing career transition coaching to many individuals in their forties and fifties. These are professionals being laid off after spending at least a decade in their organisations. Many of them perform well in their roles but are not considered capable of advancing to higher levels. These are the rusted blades—individuals who have become disposable to the organisation.

Layoffs occur for various reasons:

- Lack of opportunities for advancement
- Poor organisational performance
- Changes in the external environment that necessitate right-sizing
- Changes in strategy or the discontinuation of product/service lines, often associated with top management changes
- The need for growth at lower levels where employees are relatively 'less expensive'

These layoffs incur significant latent costs. Valuable experience and knowledge are lost, leaving remaining employees feeling insecure and worried. This can lead to decreased motivation, negative feedback in the marketplace, and dwindling trust in management.

On the other hand, the experience and knowledge of these rusted blades may no longer be relevant. They might struggle to adapt, and their presence could be demotivating to others.

To avoid or minimise such situations, several steps can be taken, though I have observed that they often are not. Here are some insights from individuals during our discussions:

1. Provide Clear Feedback: It is essential to communicate clearly the qualities needed for advancement. Employees

should be given a year to demonstrate these qualities, and feedback should ideally be delivered by someone a few levels higher in a personal and caring manner. Often, the feedback given is general. For example, one employee from a global MNC said, "I was told that I did not have enough presence and was not collaborative enough. However, these points were never mentioned in my previous appraisal discussions. When I asked for more specific details, there were none. I didn't know what was expected of me."

2. Grow Them: Professionals in their forties and fifties also need opportunities for growth. They may be excellent functional specialists or wonderful team members who have achieved stellar results, yet they may not be ready for promotion. They require support and opportunities for development beyond their current roles. In one instance, I worked with a senior leader in a consulting organisation, where a key development area identified was futuristic—relevant at the next levels. However, the sponsor and HR were particularly opposed to this development goal and actively discouraged focusing on futuristic skills. They just emphasised day to day performance. In an environment dominated by quarterly targets, long-term development often takes a backseat. Eventually, the gaps in skills and knowledge become evident.
3. Share Growth Plans: I also worked with a very senior employee in a global organisation who had previously been an A-level performer but faced an abrupt end to her role when the company decided to close its operations in India. Although the organisation wanted to retrain her for a new role abroad, she had just invested in life plans specific to India. Her repeated comment

was: "I wish I had known about this six month earlier." Ultimately, she left the organisation. Often, companies have growth plans but are reluctant to share them, leaving even high-performing employees in the dark and forcing them to leave.

4. Rationalise the Cost: Many of the individuals I have coached expressed understanding that their compensation had become high. They were open to discussing alternative compensation structures that included higher variable pay and lower fixed pay. However, these discussions seldom happen; it is simply assumed that they are "too expensive" or "inflexible".

While providing coaching support when employees are let go is valuable, it is even more beneficial when offered while they are still within the organisation. Some individuals may still need to move on, but some rusted blades may get a new lease of life.

Success, Fulfilment, and AI

What is success, in reality? This article contrasts external success with internal fulfilment, examining how AI-driven productivity may intensify the gap. It challenges readers to redefine their personal metrics, consider inner harmony, and reflect on whether their 'busy' success aligns with true satisfaction and deeper meaning.

For some time, I was contemplating sharing my thoughts on success and fulfilment. Many of my clients are immensely successful individuals, yet they do not feel fulfilled. There are a few—very few—for whom the reverse is true. I gathered some data and perspectives from various people as part of this ongoing work. Then, along came ChatGPT. Curious to experiment, I input the topics of success and fulfilment with some of the perspectives that I had collected.

I received the following response:

Success and fulfilment are two related but distinct concepts. Success generally refers to achieving a specific goal or objective, while fulfilment refers to a sense of satisfaction or meaning in one's life.

Success can be defined in many ways depending on the context. For example, in a career, success might mean earning a high salary, achieving professional recognition, or being promoted to a higher position. In sports, success might mean winning championships or setting records. In each case, success is typically measured by external markers of achievement.

Fulfilment, on the other hand, is more subjective and personal. It often involves a sense of purpose or meaning that comes from living in alignment with one's values and passions. Fulfilment can be found in various areas of life, such as relationships, creative pursuits, personal growth, and spirituality.

While success and fulfilment are not mutually exclusive, they can sometimes be at odds with each other. For example, someone may achieve great success in their career but feel unfulfilled if the work does not align with their values or passions. Conversely, someone may pursue a path of personal fulfilment without achieving any external markers of success.

Ultimately, finding a balance between success and fulfilment is a personal journey that requires self-awareness, reflection, and a willingness to make choices that align with one's values and passions.

I must say that ChatGPT captured the essence of what I wanted to convey well. To that extent, the experiment was a success. However, I do not feel a sense of fulfilment at all. This piece is crisp and comprehensive. Therefore, it may receive external validation. But there is no inner satisfaction. I also feel a sense of guilt, as if I've cheated in some way.

I suppose that is the difference between success and fulfilment.

Have you used AI in any capacity? How did you feel about it?

A Conversation with Claude.AI

This is a reflective imagined conversation with Claude.AI that nudges us to think deeply about impactful communication. Especially in scenarios with senior stakeholders. This column blurs the boundaries between the real and the reflective, prompting powerful questions about being an impactful communicator.

I am learning a lot by exploring AI options that are rapidly evolving - and enjoying the experience. Recently, I had a conversation with Claude. Claude describes itself as a next generation AI assistant. Here is a summary of our discussion. Please note that I did not instruct Claude to play the role of a coach; it was free to respond as it chose. All italicised content represents my conversation with Claude, while the rest reflects are my thoughts.

SM: I *am trying to understand how I can make my communication more impactful, especially in situations where I need to convince senior stakeholders in my organisation. I need some tips and references.*

Claude: I'll *help you develop strategies for impactful communication with senior stakeholders. Let's break this down into key principles:*

1. Start with the conclusion (BLUF - Bottom Line Up Front):

Senior leaders are time constrained.
Lead with your main point, recommendation, or request.
Follow with supporting evidence and details.
Example: "We need to invest $200K in cybersecurity upgrades to address critical vulnerabilities. Here's why..."

2. Frame around business value and strategic priorities:

Connect your message to organisational goals and metrics.
Quantify impact where possible (ROI, revenue, cost savings, risk reduction).
Show you understand their priorities and perspective.
Example: "This initiative will reduce customer churn by 15% and increase annual revenue by $2M".

3. Structure for clarity and impact:

Use the "situation, complication, resolution" framework.
Keep it concise - aim for 3-5 key points.
Anticipate and address likely questions or concerns.
Provide clear next steps or recommendations.

4. Back up assertions with evidence:

Use data, market research, and customer feedback.
Include relevant benchmarks or competitor analysis.
Share specific examples and case studies.
Avoid vague statements or unsupported claims.

5. Master non-verbal communication:

Project confidence through posture and tone.
Maintain appropriate eye contact.
Use purposeful gestures.
Match the formality level of your audience.

6. Prepare for the interaction:

Research your audience's background and interests.
Understand the decision-making process.
Have supporting materials ready.
Practise your delivery, especially for crucial presentations.
Would you like me to elaborate on any of these areas or discuss specific scenarios you're facing?

I found this advice to be very comprehensive—almost too many ideas to implement. Time-strapped professionals often need more specific guidance. To clarify my needs, I asked a more focused question, which is often explored in coaching discussions.

SM: That's *helpful. Here is my problem: I feel very unsure about how to address questions from senior people, whereas I'm comfortable with juniors. How can I tackle this issue?*

Claude: *I understand this anxiety. It's common to feel more pressure when handling questions from senior leaders. Let me break down how you can approach this more confidently:*

1. Understand why senior leaders ask questions differently:

They often ask broader, strategic questions because they're looking at the bigger picture.
For example, while juniors might ask "How does this feature work?", seniors might ask "How does this impact our market position?"

2. Common patterns in questions from senior stakeholders:

- *ROI and business impact ("What's the long-term value?")*
- *Risk assessment ("What could go wrong?")*
- *Resource implications ("What trade-offs are we making?")*
- *Strategic alignment ("How does this fit our 3-year plan?")*

3. Techniques to handle tough questions:

- *Bridge when you're not 100% sure: "That's a great question about market impact. While I don't have the exact numbers on hand, I can tell you that our pilot showed a 30% improvement in customer engagement. I can get you the detailed market analysis by tomorrow."*
- *Acknowledge complexity: "Your question touches on several aspects. Let me address the most critical part first..."*
- *Be comfortable saying "I don't know": "I need to verify the exact cost implications. I'll get that information to you within 24 hours."*

4. Preparation strategies:

> *Before any presentation, write down 3-5 challenging questions you expect.*
> *Practise answering these with a peer.*
> *Prepare key data points that senior leaders typically care about.*
> *Have a "pocket full of numbers" ready (key metrics, benchmarks).*
> *Would you like me to role-play some specific scenarios with you to practise handling questions from senior stakeholders?*

This advice felt more guided, and I noticed that Claude was open to having a lengthy conversation with a role-playing component. The standard disclaimer was also interesting—it suggested that I should double-check the responses. I wondered how I would go about that. Would I do it on ChatGPT, DeepSeek, or another platform?

Claude was eager to continue the conversation, and I was eager to process what had transpired. So, I decided to stop here.

Overall, I think expertise and insight are needed to gain better answers from AI. What I got from the conversation was exhaustive – but also a bit overwhelming.

Communicating for Impact

Communication isn't just about clarity—it's about making an impact. This article outlines simple but powerful practices to ensure your words not only convey information but also inspire action, trust, and connection.

Impactful communication is the single biggest differentiator between good leaders and outstanding ones but is one of the most underrated areas for development. Interestingly, it is also a topic that has inspired countless cartoons about poor communication. For instance, a search on Shutterstock revealed 99,927 options—from just one website!

We all communicate every day — through words, gestures, emails, and even silence. Yet how often do we pause to ask: *"Did my message truly land as I intended?"*

Look Outwards

Every meaningful conversation begins with awareness — of yourself, your listener, and the space in between.

Ask yourself:

- Do I adapt my message depending on who I'm speaking with?
- Do people find me clear and concise, or do I sometimes lose them in details?
- When emotions run high, can I stay calm and empathetic?
- Do I use eye contact, gestures, and pauses consciously?

These simple reflections open a window into your communication habits.

Because communication isn't only about *what* you say — it's about *how* you make others feel when you say it.

Look Inwards

Once you've looked outward, look inward. Your tone, adaptability, and even willingness to listen are shaped by what you believe about yourself as a communicator.

- Do you feel confident expressing ideas?
- Are you flexible enough to adapt your tone for different audiences?
- Do you pay attention to how your voice carries emotion?
- Do you seek feedback to improve — or avoid it to protect your ego?

Impactful communicators combine confidence with curiosity. They know their message has value but also recognise that every listener hears differently. That balance — of conviction and openness — is what creates resonance.

Reflect on Real Moments

Now comes the deeper work. Think about two conversations — one that went beautifully, and one that didn't. What was different?

Maybe, in the good one, you paused and truly listened. Maybe you chose the right words, or your tone carried care. In the other, perhaps emotion took over, or assumptions got in the way.

Ask yourself:

- What habits helped me connect?
- Which patterns made things worse?
- How do I usually react when misunderstood — do I clarify or defend?

Awareness grows when we stop judging and start observing.

Reflection without action is like tuning an instrument and never playing it. Once you've identified your strengths and blind spots, choose two or three areas to work on.

You might decide to pause before reacting, to summarise what others say before responding, or to pay more attention to body language. Small, consistent shifts often create the biggest impact. And if you'd like support, share your reflections or an action plan. A second pair of eyes can help you see patterns you might miss.

The Essence of Impact

At its heart, impactful communication is about eloquence and empathy.

It's not about *performing* well but about *connecting* deeply. The best communicators don't just deliver messages — they build bridges. They make others feel heard, respected, and seen.

So, take a few minutes this week to listen to yourself as carefully as you listen to others. That's where every truly impactful conversation begins.

The Manager's Toolbox

In a manager's day, every problem can feel a bit like a workshop puzzle — a jammed bolt, a loose screw, or a stuck piece of wood. The real question is: which tool do you pick up first?

The wedge helps you open resistant spaces. The hammer brings clarity and direction. The screwdriver reminds you that small, steady turns create big shifts. The chisel helps shape talent with care. And the spanner realigns the parts when teams are out of sync.

Management, after all, is not about force — it's about fit, finesse, and selecting the right tool at the right time.

There is much to learn from tools for managers. This thought came to me while discussing the qualities of a change manager with a young manager. She was assigned to head a new department, and her senior wanted to create a more dynamic department – a very broad and generic definition. The problem with such generic statements is that they are the least actionable. It's hard to know where to start or what the real objective is. So, she set out to define what "dynamic" meant to her senior and identify measurable outcomes from that definition. With some guidance from her senior, she was able to achieve this with a good level of precision.

Next came the execution, which is often where ideas go to die. The number of people who would be impacted by the proposed changes in planning methods and working processes amounted to about 250 across five sub- departments. They consisted of a diverse mix of employees from three countries, with experience levels ranging from fresh management graduates to seasoned professionals with over twenty years of experience. The sheer variety was daunting. It was soon obvious to her that there is no one tool or technique that would work for all situations. And from there, the toolbox emerged. Each tool has a unique purpose and strength, so she, as a manager, needed to sharpen her skills in different ways. Here is what she came up with:

Using **Tools as Lenses for Management Techniques**

The Wedge – Creating Entry Points for Change

Principle: Start small, go deep.
Use When: Resistance to change is high and systems are rigid.
Technique: Identify a narrow but high-leverage issue (a process, a meeting culture, a small team). Drive a small improvement

that creates visible results and use it as a proof of concept to open the door to larger change.
Manager's Action: "Find your first crack — don't fight the whole log."

It is best suited for the crusty ones with long years of experience and who are resistant to change.

The Hammer – Driving Focus and Accountability

Principle: Apply consistent pressure where it counts.
Use When: Clarity, discipline, and execution are needed.
Technique: Be firm on priorities, outcomes, and consequences. The hammer represents decisive action and setting clear boundaries.
Manager's Action: "When goals drift, bring the hammer — not to punish, but to realign."

It is useful when the pace lags or when the direction wavers for any of the changes being attempted.

The Screwdriver – Turning Incrementally

Principle: Progress through small, controlled rotations.
Use When: Precision change or cultural shift is required.
Technique: Adjust one degree at a time through feedback loops, reflection meetings, and minor course corrections.
Manager's Action: "Tighten gradually; too much torque strips the thread."

The hammer can bend the nail or damage the wall around. But the screw driver helps the screw create its own space and hold hard, ensuring everyone has time to adjust.

The Chisel – Shaping Talent and Strategy

Principle: Shape, don't shatter.
Use When: You're developing people or refining strategy.
Technique: Remove excess gently and reveal potential through coaching conversations developmental feedback, and pruning non-core activities.
Manager's Action: "Chip away at what's unnecessary to reveal the essential."

It is best for energetic fresh graduate's eager to make an impact. The chisel can shape and channel their energy effectively.

The Spanner (Wrench) – Adjusting Fit and Alignment

Principle: Connect and calibrate moving parts.
Use When: Teams, systems, or processes are out of sync.
Technique: Identify misalignments (between vision, people, or incentives) and adjust until everything fits correctly.
Manager's Action: "Don't force it — find the right size and turn until it runs smoothly."

And if one size does not fit all, then what is better than the wrench? It adjusts its own shape to make things happen effortlessly.

Putting It Together: The Manager's Toolbox

Tool	Core Skill	When to Use	Metaphoric Purpose
Wedge	Entry and leverage	Resistance or stuck change	Create a foothold
Hammer	Focus and accountability	Drifting goals or low discipline	Drive direction

Tool	Core Skill	When to Use	Metaphoric Purpose
Screwdriver	Precision and iteration	Small, cumulative change	Fine-tune systems
Chisel	Coaching and shaping	Talent or vision development	Reveal potential
Spanner	Alignment and integration	Teams out of sync	Tighten the system

Recognising and utilising these tools can significantly enhance a manager's ability to navigate the complexity of their work environment effectively.

Managing the Small, Sticky Stuff

Like glitter or sand, low-value tasks stick to you and drain your focus. Reply-all emails, vague requests, urgent requests, and endless administrative work create the illusion of productivity but block strategic impact. Breaking free needs prioritisation, boundaries, delegation, and mindfulness so that you can move from being busy to being truly impactful.

What do glitter, sand, chewing gum, and honey have in common? They are all sticky substances that do not easily go away. Similarly, endless reply-all email chains, vague inquiries labelled as "quick questions", repetitive client queries, meeting invites with unclear purposes, and urgent requests fluttering in and out like fireflies also do not disappear unless you actively deal with them.

Every seasoned coach has witnessed this familiar pattern: managers, despite their best intentions and training, often find themselves ensnared in a web of minor "C category" tasks. These low-priority items—nagging emails, quick requests, and recurring administrative chores—consume valuable hours, leaving little room for the strategic, high-impact work that defines effective leadership.

This phenomenon is not simply a quirk of personality or a failure of willpower. The "stickiness" of small tasks is the result of deep-seated psychological tendencies, organisational pressures, and cultural norms. For managers to "unglue" themselves from the trivial and step boldly into their true value-adding roles, they must first understand why minor tasks feel so compelling.

1. The Illusion of Productivity

Completing small tasks delivers a quick hit of satisfaction. Crossing items off a list, responding promptly to messages, and making routine decisions all provide an immediate sense of accomplishment. This feeling can be addictive—a dopamine-driven cycle where visible results are mistaken for meaningful progress.

The allure is especially strong in environments where "busyness" is equated with worth. Managers might even fear judgement or diminished status if their time does not appear fully occupied by tangible activity, regardless of how inconsequential that activity is.

2. Avoidance of Discomfort and Uncertainty

Strategic, high-priority work—the "A category"—is often ambiguous, complex, or politically sensitive. It requires deep focus, creative thinking, and a willingness to confront failure. In contrast, minor tasks are typically straightforward, clear-cut, and low-risk. When managers feel overwhelmed or uncertain, retreating into the comfort zone of minor tasks provides an easy way to regain a sense of control.

3. The Demands of a Reactive Culture

Many organisations reward responsiveness over results. Managers are praised for being available, quickly answering emails, and ensuring no detail slips through the cracks. This creates a culture of reactivity, where proactivity is stifled by a constant stream of urgent but unimportant tasks. Over time, managers internalise this expectation, training themselves to prioritise whatever is immediately in front of them.

4. The Myth of Multitasking

There is a persistent belief that effective managers should be able to juggle multiple tasks with ease. In practice, frequent task-switching undermines focus and diminishes work quality. Small tasks provide the illusion that multitasking is effective because they are simple to complete and seem not to interfere with larger projects—until one realises that the larger projects are stalled.

5. Fear of Letting Others Down

Especially for newer managers, saying "no" or delegating lower-priority tasks can feel risky. There is a fear of being perceived as unhelpful or disengaged. Consequently, managers may overcommit to minor requests at the expense of their most important goals.

Escaping the stickiness of low-priority work is not a matter of simply trying harder or working longer hours; it requires deliberate changes in mindset, habits, and potentially even organisational systems. Here are some strategies that have proven effective for others. Feel free to choose one or more that resonate with you.

1. Ruthlessly Prioritise Using the Eisenhower Matrix

The Eisenhower Matrix is a powerful tool for distinguishing between what is urgent and what is important. By regularly mapping tasks into four quadrants—important and urgent, important but not urgent, not important but urgent, and not important and not urgent—managers can increase their awareness of how much time they spend on "C category" tasks (not important, regardless of urgency). This awareness is the first step toward meaningful change.

- Schedule regular reviews (daily or weekly) to categorise tasks and ruthlessly delegate, defer, or delete "C category" items.
- Use your calendar to protect time for "A category" work before the day begins, rather than after completing smaller tasks.

2. Set Clear Boundaries and Communicate Them

Managers who are always available for every small request train their teams, peers, and superiors to expect instant responses. Setting boundaries is not selfish; it is essential. This may include:

- Designating "deep work" time on your calendar when you are not available for meetings or emails.
- Using auto-responders or status indicators to inform others when you will respond.
- Proactively informing colleagues of your focus priorities and preferred communication channels for urgent issues.

3. Delegate with Confidence

Delegation is a hallmark of effective management, yet many avoid it for fear of burdening others or losing control. To delegate well:

- Align tasks with team members' developmental goals, making delegation mutually beneficial.
- Provide clear expectations and necessary resources, but avoid micromanaging.
- Celebrate team members' successes in handling delegated work to reinforce positive behaviour.

4. Embrace "No" as a Strategic Tool

Saying "no" does not indicate a lack of helpfulness; it demonstrates intentionality. Practise polite but firm ways to decline or defer requests that do not align with your priorities. For example:

- "I'm currently focused on [priority project]; would you like me to connect you with someone else who can assist?"

- "I'd love to help, but my schedule is fully committed this week. Can we revisit this next month?"

5. Design Systems to Minimise Distraction

While small tasks will always arise, systems can minimise their disruptive impact.

- Group administrative or routine tasks into designated time slots, rather than addressing them as they arise.
- Leverage technology for filtering and automating routine communications—email rules, templates, and delegation tools can be beneficial.
- Regularly audit your commitments and eliminate unnecessary recurring meetings or reports.

6. Develop Reflective and Mindful Practices

Self-awareness is the antidote to unconscious busyness. Mindfulness practices, such as brief check-ins at the start and end of each day, can help you recognise when you are slipping into a reactive mode and then intentionally reset your focus.

The journey from busy to impactful is ongoing, requiring regular reflection and adaptation. Each step taken away from trivial tasks brings you closer to the core responsibilities of leadership: shaping the future, developing others, and driving meaningful progress.

The First Listener

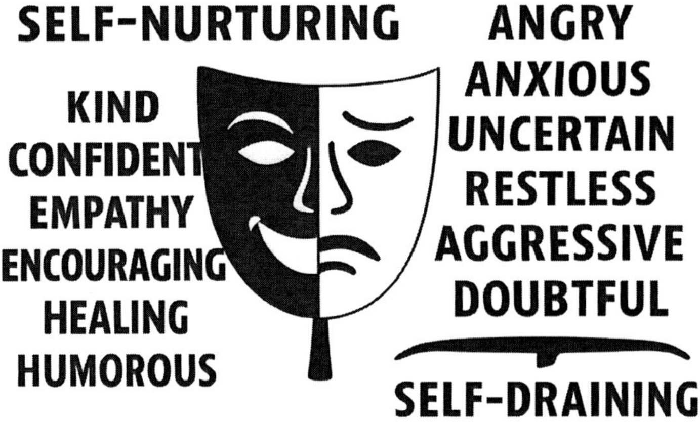

Our words don't just communicate outwardly; they also echo inwardly. This has significant implications for your self-awareness, confidence, and emotional well-being. While you often strive to listen better to others, you frequently neglect to listen to yourself. Most of the time, you operate on autopilot.

Who is the first person who hears your words? It is you. Many times, you may not even articulate your thoughts, which means no one else has heard them. However, you are in a constant conversation with yourself all day long. Your words shape not only your external world but also your internal world. Being mindful of your words is essential, as they shape your perception, moods, beliefs, and future choices. Therefore, it is essential to be conscious of what you say.

Here is a table outlining the impact of your words on you, your self-image, and your relationships, along with a representative chart illustrating their nurturing or draining effects.

If your words/ tone are	*Impact on you*	*Impact on your image*	*Impact on Relationships*
Angry	*Heightens stress, frustration, guilt afterward*	*Seen as volatile or unsafe*	*Creates fear, conflict, withdrawal*
Aggressive	*Leads to short-term dominance, long-term anxiety or shame*	*Viewed as harsh or domineering*	*Pushes people away, creates defensiveness*
Empathetic	*Promotes calmness, connection, emotional balance*	*Seen as warm, wise, collaborative*	*Builds trust, openness, and respect*
Apologetic	*Releases guilt, invites resolution*	*Respected for maturity and honesty*	*Repairs trust, diffuses tension*

If your words/ tone are	*Impact on you*	*Impact on your image*	*Impact on Relationships*
Humorous	*Lightens mood, reduces stress*	*Seen as approachable and clever (if appropriate)*	*Builds rapport and ease*
Sympathetic	*Evokes care, warmth, sometimes sadness*	*Viewed as compassionate and understanding*	*Builds closeness, emotional support*
Wise	*Encourages reflection, clarity, inner calm*	*Respected as thoughtful and insightful*	*Inspires others, earns trust*
Encouraging	*Boosts optimism, energises motivation*	*Seen as supportive and empowering*	*Strengthens bonds, inspires action*
Doubtful	*Creates uncertainty, drains confidence*	*Seen as hesitant, unconvincing, or lacking direction*	*Weakens trust and decision-making clarity*
Sarcastic	*Creates momentary amusement or superiority, but may breed cynicism*	*Seen as witty by some, cutting or dismissive by others*	*Can alienate, confuse, or hurt others*

Impact of your words/tone on you - Self-Nurturing vs. Self-Draining

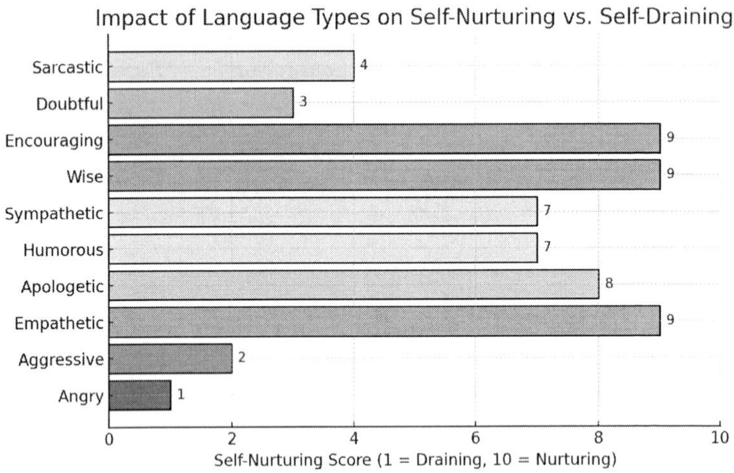

Becoming More Conscious as You Speak

The important question is: what can you do to incorporate more mindful communication? Start by slowing down your speech. Create a parallel thought track to observe what is happening within you as you speak. Are your words capturing your thoughts accurately? Are you becoming agitated? Are you speaking merely to make a point or to defend a previous statement? Are you trying to win the argument, or are you aiming for a meaningful conversation? Do you feel in control of the dialogue, or are you getting sucked into the quicksand of the interaction? Are you feeling calm and able to choose your words carefully, or are they just pouring out?

As you become more aware of the impact of your words on yourself, the quality of your communication will improve—becoming clearer, more empathetic, and more solution- oriented.

If you find that you missed the opportunity to observe during the conversation, you can always take a pause and reflect. Are you feeling tension, shame, anger, or guilt? Or are you feeling light, satisfied, calm, and constrictive? If you experience the former emotions, your words may have hurt you—perhaps even more than they may have hurt others. There's a good chance the impact of your words was not positive. Conversely, if you feel the latter emotions, it's likely that your words were empowering and kind, positively influencing the conversation.

When you pause, treat yourself as someone worth listening to. Avoid self-judgment—don't say, "I am such an idiot." Instead, be curious: "That didn't go too well. I wonder what triggered my reaction?" or "How could I have expressed this better?"

Final Thought

Becoming a **conscious, compassionate listener** to your own words lays the foundation for emotional intelligence, confidence, and inner leadership.

Can you be your own observer?

Post-Reaction Recovery

Reactions are a fundamental aspect of being human. The challenge is not the reactions themselves; it's when we become trapped in them. The key lies in the process of recovery: taking a moment before becoming consumed by the reaction, accepting the situation without resistance, opting for inquiries rather than justifications, offering apologies when appropriate, realigning our mindset, and engaging in introspection.

We've all heard the phrase, "Respond, don't react." It is easy to say, but hard to practise. The truth is, everyone reacts—sometimes due to ego, sometimes because of conflicting values, and sometimes simply because we are human and tired. What truly matters is what happens **after** the reaction. Do we let it spiral out of control, or do we recover, reset, and repair?

Here are some illustrative stories about what recovery can look like. The names are fictitious, but the situations are real. In each case, two essential elements are involved: managing the mind and finding the right words.

Pause and Give Yourself Breathing Space

Ravi was in the middle of a project review when one of his junior colleagues challenged his numbers. Already under pressure from tight deadlines, Ravi snapped:

"If you'd actually done your homework, you'd know these figures are correct."

The room went quiet, and Ravi immediately sensed the shift — his words had landed harder than intended. He was tempted to continue defending himself, but something stopped him. Instead, he excused himself:

"Give me a minute; I'll be right back."

He walked to the coffee machine, took three slow breaths, and stared out the window. It wasn't about the numbers; it was about him feeling undermined. Ten minutes later, he returned calmer and said,

"Let's review those figures together — maybe I can explain them better."

By creating space for himself, he halted the downward spiral, allowing the meeting to proceed without further escalation.

Acknowledge, Without Over-Explaining

Meera was out at dinner with close friends. One of them teased her for being "fashionably late" — a running joke in the group. Exhausted from a long day, she snapped:

"At least I show up, unlike some people."

The laughter died down instantly. She could see her friends stiffen. In that moment, she had two choices: pretend her comment meant nothing, or try to justify her outburst. Instead, she simply said:

"Sorry, that came out sharper than I intended. I'm just drained."

She kept it brief, avoiding lengthy explanations about traffic, deadlines, or exhaustion. The table relaxed again, and the conversation moved on, saving the evening.

Sometimes, a short acknowledgment is all it takes to bring the temperature down.

Switch From Ego to Curiosity

During a brainstorming session, Ankit pitched an idea he'd been refining for weeks. His manager dismissed it in just two lines:

"This is too complicated. Let's move on."

Ankit felt stung. His first impulse was to push back:

"You haven't even listened to me properly!"

However, he refrained from doing so. Later, instead of defending himself, he asked his manager privately:

"Hey, I noticed you felt my idea wouldn't work. Could you tell me more about what seemed impractical?"

The manager explained that the concern wasn't about the idea itself but about budget implications:

"It's strong, but we can't fund it this quarter."

By choosing curiosity over ego, Ankit discovered it wasn't personal at all. And because he hadn't argued, the manager later circled back to say:

"Let's revisit this in the next cycle. Don't drop it — it has potential."

willingness to listen kept the door open.

Repair and Reframe

Rina was leading a tense client call. Frustrated by repeated delays, she blurted out:

"Frankly, your team's inefficiency is holding us back."

The silence on the line indicated she'd crossed a line. The call ended awkwardly. That night, she replayed the conversation in her head and realised the potential damage to the relationship.

The next morning, she sent a short, sincere note:

"I realise I came across as harsh yesterday. I let my frustration get the better of me, and I'm sorry for that. Let's focus on how we can move things forward together."

To her relief, the client responded warmly:

"We appreciate your honesty. Let's regroup with clearer timelines."

Instead of eroding trust, her quick repair and reframing deepened the partnership.

Reset Yourself Emotionally

After a heated argument with his teenage son about grades, Suresh stormed into his room, replaying his words:

"You're wasting your potential!"

Guilt set in almost instantly. However, he knew staying stuck in guilt would only widen the gap between them. So, he stepped outside for a walk, practising a grounding exercise: he focused on the rustle of leaves, the smell of food from a nearby stall, and the sound of a passing scooter. Slowly, his chest unclenched.

When he returned home, he knocked on his son's door and said:

"I overreacted earlier. Can we talk again?"

This time, the conversation was calmer. Resetting himself emotionally helped him repair their bond instead of letting the argument fester.

Build Your Recovery Muscle

Priya, a team leader, noticed a pattern: she often snapped at colleagues during late-evening meetings. She decided to track her reactions in a small "reaction journal". Each entry included three aspects: what triggered her, how she felt in her body, and what actions she took afterward.

After a few weeks, she recognised recurring themes: tiredness, feeling ignored, and pressure to "wrap things up quickly". With this awareness, she inculcated a new habit. Before any late meeting, she'd pause and ask herself:

"Am I tired today? How should I handle discussions today?"

These simple questions reduced her reactivity dramatically. When she did slip up, she was quicker to acknowledge it and bounce back. Her colleagues even noticed the change, with one saying:

"You've become calmer lately. Meetings feel lighter."

This practice of reflection had strengthened her recovery muscle.

The Key

Reactions are a natural part of being human. They're not the problem — it's staying stuck in them that creates issues. What matters most is recovery: pausing before you spiral, acknowledging without defensiveness, asking questions instead of defending yourself, apologising when needed, resetting emotionally, and practising self-reflection.

Tanya's Legacy

This is a complex question and a deep need for many individuals. More than just a remembrance, it's a reflection on how character and kindness shape memories long after titles fade.

A few days ago, I was having a coaching conversation—just the second to last discussion we were having. Let us call the coachee Tanya.

Tanya suddenly said, "I want to discuss something new today." I waited for her to continue. After a brief pause, she hesitatingly added, "I want to leave a legacy." This was a novel request, as it's not a common topic in coaching programmes, even though it may be a deep desire for many.

Here's how the conversation unfolded, roughly:

Me: Interesting. Many of us would like that, but what does legacy mean to you?

Tanya: I would like for eight or nine out of ten people who meet me to remember me. Right now, maybe only two or three do.

Me: Remember you for what?

Tanya: Hmmm. For being a good person?

Me: Anything else?

Tanya: It would be good if I could create life-changing events for some of them. That would be very satisfying.

Me: What would you say is your fundamental motivation for leaving behind a legacy? Do you want people to remember you, which might feed your ego, or do you want to feel satisfied?

Tanya: I am not sure. Maybe both.

Me: Okay. That sounds good. How would you like to be remembered? Let's try to sum it up in five words.

Tanya: Good person, helpful manager, competent, result-oriented, strategic?

Me: Are those words too generic? People tend to remember only the exceptional qualities. What do you think is exceptional about you?

Tanya: Hmmm. I've never thought about it.

Me: Alright. Let us look at the other interesting thing you said. You want to change lives. Can you think of a couple of things done by others that changed your life?

Tanya: I can't think of any right now, but I'm sure some things have happened. They will come back to me.

Me: Another question has popped into my mind. What do we need to do before we leave something behind for others?

Tanya: I don't know. I try to be a good manager, and I receive good reviews from people. But that does not seem like enough for a legacy.

Me: That makes sense. Leaving a legacy does seem more significant than just being a good manager. I am thinking of people who have left some mark on us. Were they planning to leave a mark, or were they simply doing what they thought was right?

Tanya: True. So is there something more fundamental here?

Me: That is something to discover, I guess. You have generated a lot of food for thought here. Leaving a legacy behind seems different from just being a good person or doing a great job.

Tanya: It seems I need to give this some more thought.

Me: That sounds good.

We continued the conversation for some more time and revisited the topic a couple of times. Here are the thoughts that emerged:

- Many, if not all of us, want to leave a legacy behind.
- Most of us are not clear about what this means; we cannot define it clearly.
- To leave something behind, we first must build something. It can be a financial empire, works of art, and revolutionary thoughts, along with instilling good values in others, writing books, and more. All these can be valid legacies.
- To leave a sustainable, memorable, and impactful legacy, we may have to go beyond the obvious—beyond what many others are doing.
- Leaving a legacy can be a conscious decision, a planned one, or it can simply happen as a byproduct of how we live. Either way, it involves diligently working on something and consistently displaying certain values over the years. Legacies can be large or small. Opening a dog shelter can be a legacy; planting a hundred trees can be a legacy; setting up a corporation can be a legacy. It is also okay to not leave any legacy—fading away into the sunset is perfectly fine.

Though there is no single way to create a legacy, there are some guidelines:

1. Focus on Excellence: Excellence tends to stand out and be remembered.
2. Innovate: Innovation often leaves a lasting mark.
3. Mentor and Inspire Others: Sharing knowledge helps shape the future and ensures your impact continues through others.

4. Build Strong Relationships: Positive relationships can extend the influence of your work.
5. Document Your Work: Documenting your work makes it easier for others to understand and build upon it.
6. Create Value: Work that creates real value tends to be remembered.
7. Share Your Story: Sharing your story can inspire others and ensure that your contributions are recognised.
8. Contribute to the Community: Being an active contributor can amplify your impact.

This is one exam whose result we will never come to know. Until we are gone, our legacies are a work in progress. Tanya has identified what she would like to leave as her legacy, and it, too, is a work in progress.

As often happens with such conversations, this one stirred something deep within me. It made me reflect on my own legacy, which is also a work in progress.

Index of Thematic Ideas

Here is a thematic index of the key concepts, patterns, and leadership messages across the book. This will help you locate specific topics of interest.

You can also get a pdf workbook with self-reflection questions, action steps and awareness check for each chapter. Please send a mail to shyam@pobox.com with subject line Thematic Ideas if you would like to get this.

1. Mindset & Inner Patterns

Themes about inner orientation, limiting beliefs, cognitive filters, and personal growth.

- **Mindsets (Limiting & Liberating)** – abundance vs scarcity, solution vs problem, climb vs cruise, victim vs creator, owner vs worker (Ch. 2 *Mind Your Mindset*, pp. 3–11)
- **Belief Systems & Reality Alignment** – conviction vs realism, balancing passion with practicality (Ch. 1 *Belief and Reality*, pp. 1–2)
- **Being Judgemental vs Exercising Judgement** – causes of judgement, self-righteousness, perception traps (Ch. 3, pp. 12–14)
- **Self-Sabotaging Patterns** – recurring internal derailers (Ch. 39 *Top Ten Self-Saboteurs*)
- **Regret, Envy & Revenge as Hidden Drivers** (Ch. 6 *To Err is Human*, pp. 24–27)
- **The Stuck Needle (Gramophone)** – breaking repetitive mental grooves

2. Emotional Mastery & Self-Regulation

Themes that explore feelings, emotional triggers, presence, and self-management.

- **Handling Envy, Revenge, Regret** – emotional undercurrents that drive outward behaviour (Ch. 6, pp. 25–27)
- **Presence & Mindfulness**
  - Attached Observer – sensing without being swept away (Ch. 7, pp. 28–30)
  - Building Presence – awareness of mindspace vs timespace (Ch. 14)
- **Stress & Anxiety**
  - The Stress Virus – how emotional contagion spreads (Ch. 33)
  - Blues at Fifty – emotional transitions of midlife (Ch. 31)
- **Feelings as Signals** – emoticons of inner state (Ch. 44)
- **Stool of Upsets** – three-legged model for emotional triggers (Ch. 40)
- **Post-Reaction Recovery** – skill of returning to equilibrium after a trigger (Ch. 53)

3. Leadership Identity & Avatars

Themes for understanding the *self for leadership.*

- **Leadership Avatars** – 23 behavioural archetypes (Ch. 10 & 37, pp. 37–43)
- **The Cheetah & The Chameleon** – agility and adaptability (Ch. 11, pp. 44–46)
- **River, Dam & Leadership** – flow vs resistance (Ch. 13)
- **The Rock & Banyan Tree** – stability and interconnectedness (Ch. 37)
- **The Clone** – losing originality in organisations (Ch. 36)

4. Decision-Making & Judgement

Ideas related to clarity, choices, uncertainty, risk, and intuition.

- **The Myth of the Right Decision** – no perfect choices exist (Ch. 27)
- **Making the Decision Right** – commitment after choosing (Ch. 28)
- **Intuition Harnessing** – nurturing instinct in low-data situations (Ch. 9, pp. 34–36)
- **Risk vs Security Orientation** – mindsets toward uncertainty (Ch. 2 excerpts)

5. Communication, Influence & Presence

Themes related to impact, conversations, visibility, and influence.

- **Talk the Walk** – communicating achievements with humility (Ch. 12, pp. 47–50)
- **Curious & Concerned** – empathy in action via behaviour (Ch. 8, pp. 31–33)
- **Mirror, Mirror** – self-awareness through feedback (Ch. 18)
- **Impactful Communication** – landing meaningfully with others (Ch. 49)
- **The First Listener** – how one's inner voice shapes outward speech (Ch. 52)

6. Relationships, Teams & Stakeholders

Interpersonal dynamics, peer management, judgement, expectations.

- **Difficult Conversations** – frames for clarity & courage (Ch. 35)
- **The Art of Peer Management** – influence without authority (Ch. 38)

- **Master of Expectation Management** – balancing what others expect vs what you deliver (Ch. 17)
- **Judgemental vs Understanding Modes** – relational impact (Ch. 3)
- **Senior Presence (Tanya's Challenge)** – decoding upward influence (Ch. 41)

7. Career Transitions & Growth Navigation

Themes around mid-career shifts, the 40s–50s transition, and professional reinvention.

- **Avoiding the Trim List** (Ch. 4, pp. 15–18)
- **Caught in the Trim List** – navigating layoffs (Ch. 5, pp. 19–23)
- **Resume Plus** – reframing your professional narrative (Ch. 20)
- **Twists, Turns & Success** – nonlinear career journeys (Ch. 26)
- **Blues at Fifty** – emotional & cognitive fog of midlife (Ch. 31)

8. Change, Agility & Adaptability

How leaders respond to volatility, ambiguity, uncertainty.

- **Agility & Adaptability (Cheetah & Chameleon)** – fast movement + sensitive adjustment (Ch. 11)
- **TsunAmI** – sudden unexpected shocks (Ch. 32)
- **Rusty Blades** – skills that have dulled over time (Ch. 46)
- **Growing the Box** – expanding the frame within which you operate (Ch. 22)

9. Purpose, Fulfilment & Meaning

Ideas touching the "inner journey of leadership."

- **Success vs Fulfilment** – redefining achievement (Ch. 47)

- **Let Go – But of What?** – releasing attachment to ego, struggle, roles (Ch. 19)
- **Power of Acceptance** – finding peace in reality (Ch. 21)
- **Tanya's Legacy** – leadership lessons that outlast the role (Ch. 54)

10. Tools, Frameworks & Practical Methods

Usable exercises, models, and templates that appear throughout the book.

- **Trim List** – mid-career stagnation filter (Ch. 4–5)
- **Mindset Questions** – self-inquiry framework (Ch. 2)
- **Expectation Stool / Stool of Upsets** – identifying emotional triggers (Ch. 40)
- **Manager's Toolbox** – practical levers for day-to-day leadership (Ch. 50)
- **Sticky Stuff (Managing the Small Things)** – clutter, unresolved items, micro-irritants (Ch. 51)
- **PVR & Drama Triangle** – Persecutor–Victim–Rescuer shifts (Ch. 42)